Varṇa Vidyā

The Biological Basis of Varṇa Dharma,
especially for **Women & the Śūdra Varṇa**

Sinu Joseph

ISBN 979-8-89133-905-7

Contents

Cover Page Painting

The image on the cover page of this book is from an original painting of Śrī Lalitāmbika Devī, which happened through the author during Śāradīya Navarātri 2023, after completing the manuscript of this book. The painting is influenced by the Kerala mural style and is based on the dhyāna sloka-s of Devī as per the Lalitā Sahasranāma.

It is recommended that readers meditate upon this form of Devī and seek Her anugraha to be able to fully understand the subtle meaning of what is conveyed in this work.

Sanskrit Pronunciation Guide

In this book, the International Alphabet of Sanskrit Transliteration (IAST) has been used for words and names that were originally in Sanskrit (henceforth written as *Saṃskṛtam*), even though some of the words like chakra, karma or mantra might have become part of the English language in recent times. However, in cases where the author quotes another source, the spelling and style given in the source might have been retained. The plurals of saṃskṛtam words have been indicated with a hyphen followed by 's.' For example, śāstra-s, mantra-s, Veda-s, etc. The pronunciations as per IAST are given below:

a	u in but	*ḍa*	d in dust
ā	a in star	*ḍha*	dh in adhere
i	i in bit	*ṇa*	n in under
ī	ee in teeth	*ta*	t in thumb
u	u in put	*tha*	aspirated ta
ū	oo in mood	*da*	th in the
ṛ	r in rough	*dha*	aspirated da
ṝ	longer ṛ	*na*	n in not
e	a in mane	*pa*	p in spill
o	o in go	*pha*	p in pill
ō	o in odour	*ba*	b in bill
ai	combination of a and i	*bha*	aspirated b
au	combination of a and u	*ma*	m in mail
ka	k in skill	*ya*	y in yellow

kh	kh in khakhi	*ra*	r in run
ga	g in gun	*la*	l in light
gha	gh in Ghana	*va*	v in vase
ṅa	ng in lung	*śa*	s in shine
ca	c in inch	*ṣa*	s in push
cha	c in church	*sa*	s in see
ja	j in jug	*ha*	voiced h
jha	j in Jhansi	*aṃ*	Sum
ña	n in lunch	*aḥ*	Aha
ṭa	t in time	*jña*	Gnya
ṭha	th in anthill	*hma, hna*	mha, nha

Some of the frequently used words in this book and their IAST forms
are as follows:

rishi – ṛṣi; rishika – ṛṣika; krishna – kṛṣṇa; shastra – śāstra; shree –
śrī; chakra – cakra

Preface

Mahāperiyavā śaraṇaṃ

In this land of saints, there lived a Great One in recent times, who was an authority on the Veda and śāstra and was considered an avatar of Bhagavān himself—His Holiness Jagadguru Śrī Chandraśekharendra Saraswathi Swamigal (1894–1994), the 68th Pīṭhādhipathi of Śrī Kānchi Kāmakoṭi pīṭham. To millions of devotees, he was simply Periyavā—the revered one, or Mahāperiyavā, a term that conveys the reverence, affection and devotion of millions of people towards the great Swamigal. His talks, captured in a series of essays called Deivathin Kural (in Tamil) and translated into English as 'Voice of God', have been my primary source of reference for understanding the intent behind the rules pertaining to the śāstra-s. Mahāperiyavā's in-depth and experiential knowledge of the śāstra is easily missed if we are distracted by his utter

humility characterising his explanation of the reasons for niyama-s (rules), as he always refers to himself as one among the masses. In spite of the difficulty of the times he lived in, when the government and even Hindu devotees were making the shift to secular and liberal thinking, Periyavā's teachings stuck to the śāstra, never apologetic, never compromising, in the hope that someday people would see the sense in it and return to the original way. Therefore, it feels right that we begin this work by taking a look at what Mahāperiyavā said with reference to varṇa and jāti.

Varṇa and Jāti

Periyavā says that although in colloquial language, we often refer to varṇa and jāti interchangeably, the two are not the same. Within each varṇa, there are several jāti-s. Quoting Periyavā's words:

> "There are four varṇa-s: brāhmaṇa, kṣatriya, vaiśya and śūdra. Within each, there are many jāti-s. Among brāhmaṇa, there are Ayyars, Ayyangars, Raos, and so on. In the fourth varṇa, there are Mudaliars, Pillais, Reddis, Naikkars, Nayadus, Gaundars and Padayachis. In common parlance, jāti is used for varṇa.

> The śāstra-s lay down separate rites and practices for the four jāti-s (that is the four varṇa-s). This means that within the fold of the same religion, Hinduism, there are numerous differences. Food cooked by one is not to be eaten by another. A young man belonging to one jāti is not to marry a girl belonging to another. The vocation practised by one jāti is not to be practised by another. The differences are indeed far too many.

> What one man does as part of his dharma (such as wearing the sacred thread and chanting) is considered as adharma for another. The reverse is also true, in the sense that if the person who chants the Veda-s does not bathe and keep his stomach empty, he will be guilty of adharma. Another, however, need not necessarily bathe nor observe fasts. For some it is an offence to chant the Veda-s, while for others it is an offence not to chant."[1]

---

1 Voice of God, Vol 2. Chapter: Jathis – why so many differences?

Periyavā speaks about the opinion of many Hindu-s who quote the Gīta saying that Śri Kṛṣṇa Paramāthmā says that the vocations are assigned to people according to the difference in their nature, and not according to their birth. He then proceeds to examine these assumptions in the below passages:

"Let us first consider the view that according to the Veda-s themselves jāti is not based on birth. (After all, the Veda-s are the source of our religion, so it is essential to be clear on this point). The present contention about what the Veda-s say about jāti is based on a passage read out of context. What is mentioned as an exception to the rule is being interpreted as the rule itself. I will give firm proof that jāti is based on birth and not on the nature and quality of individuals. The chaula of children belonging to a particular jāti is performed at the age of three, the upanayana at five or seven. These are saṃskāra-s based on birth and performed in childhood. So, it would be absurd to claim that one's vocation is based on one's nature of qualities. Is it possible to determine one's qualities or nature in early childhood?

Let us now come to Gīta. It is true that the Gīta speaks of 'samadarśana', seeing the self-same thing in everything and everybody. But it would be perverse to argue on this basis that the Gīta does not recognise any jāti distinctions. When, according to Kṛṣṇa, do we attain the stage of 'samathva', the stage when we will look upon all as equal? We must consider the context. The Lord speaks of samadarśana of the wise man who is absorbed in the ātman and for whom there exists nothing (other than the ātman) — and even the fact that Iśwara is the creator is of no consequence to him. The Lord says that all are equal for a man when he renounces karma entirely to become an ascetic and attains the final state of enlightenment. The Veda-s and the upaniṣad-s say the same thing. Only an individual belonging to the highest plane can see all things as One (as one Reality). Samadarśana is not of this phenomenal world of plurality nor is it for us who are engaged in works. The Lord speaks in the Gītā of samadarśana, samachiththa and samabhuddhi from the yogin's point of view, but by no means does he refer to samakāryathva as applied to our worldly existence."[2]

In the above paragraph, Mahāperiyavā makes a very important point that the rules of varṇa do not apply to one who has become united with the ātman, but we must not make the error of using this exception and applying to all those who still identify with the body and are engaged in saṃsāra (worldly, material pursuits).

At this point, it is probably necessary to mention what Periyavā meant by "by birth". In a widely shared audio message by a devotee, there is the mention of a recorded incident of a Russian named Professor Ribakov, who wanted to meet Periyavā and came all the way to Tamil Nadu to meet him. The Russian had several questions to ask Periyavā, but the moment he got the opportunity to stand in front of Periyavā, all his questions vanished, and he went silent at the sight of Periyavā. To his surprise, Periyavā asked him, "Russians speak their language mixed with Saṃskṛtaṃ, but in Northern Russia, do they speak the language without any mix of Saṃskṛtaṃ?" Ribakov was surprised and replied, "Yes." Then Periyavā said, "You say Russia now. In the ancient times, it was known as Rishivarsham. You know why? That is where ṛṣi-s like Yājñavalkya were running a Vedic Research Centre." Then, he spoke about the history of Russia at length.

After listening to Periyavā, the Russian was so moved that he told Periyavā, "I want to become a Hindu." To this, Periyavā replied, "You already are a Hindu." And then Periyavā went on to say that every human is a Hindu by birth. It is a human intervention, such as baptism for Christians or similar purification rituals in Islam and among Jews, that gives them a different man-made identity.

---

2 Voice of God, Volume 2: Jathi according to the Veda-s and the Gita

So, when Periyavā says that varṇā and jāti are by birth, shouldn't that also be understood as applicable to all humans and not just Hindu-s? It is just that the Hindu-s evolved enough to recognise this and come up with a way of living based on it. In the absence of the organisation of varṇa-s as seen among Hindu-s, an ordinary person might not be able to readily know their or another person's varṇa, but that does not mean that it doesn't exist. For those who think of varṇa and jāti as mere social constructs within Hinduism, this would be quite confusing. But the truth that Periyavā knew, that the Veda-s and śāstra-s declared (and that which is also the subject matter of this book) is that varṇa is a biological phenomenon, applicable to all humans. The only difference is that Hindu-s have kept track of it by following the varṇa sampradāya, unlike others.

Nature vs Nurture

In the Western world, there is always the debate about nature versus nurture. The question of whether individuals are born a certain way (e.g., born leaders) or if they can be trained to be that way (what all the management and business schools claim to do) is something many intellectuals debate. When we understand varṇa and jāti for what they are, we might find answers to this.

If varṇa is nature, jāti is nurture. In the earlier days, when marriages were carefully planned among people of the same jāti and varṇa, there was no confusion as to what the child would pursue by way of a living. The jāti would ensure that the vocation would be in tune with the sādhanā (practice in the spiritual path) required for that person as per the varṇa. Thus, the natural qualities that lie dormant in the person of that varṇa would be awakened by the vocation prescribed for that jāti. The absence of this organised way of living based on biology is the reason why many of us pursue career paths that do not make us happy, as it is out of tune with our inherent personality and natural ability.

Often, youngsters ask the question, 'How do we maintain a work-life balance?' The answer is that if we know our svadharma, there must be no difference between our work and life. It is by realising one's varṇa and pursuing work in accordance with one's jāti, that both material and spiritual fulfilment can be obtained. For example, brāhmaṇa men who pursue the materialistic way of living and feel dissatisfied. Their ātma is always seeking something that their way of living is unable to provide. Some of them, towards the end of their life, take to the study of the Veda-s and realise that this was the purpose of their birth, their svadharma. If they (and their parents & grandparents) had followed their varṇa dharma and jāti dharma and guided their children to do the same, much of the restlessness, the distractions of worldly pursuits, and the resulting accumulation of new karma could have been avoided.

The ātma is always aware of why it has taken birth in a given form. It could take several lifetimes before the character that we consider ourselves to be recognises itself as one with the ātma. Until that happens, would it not have been nice if we, the character, could know what the purpose of the ātma, our svadharma, is in each birth? Would it not have saved us so much time, heartbreak and suffering as we go around in circles before we find our purpose in life? Well, that is what true knowledge of varṇa dharma can do.

Parāśara Smṛti[3] says, 'Know that to be dharma which is pronounced by three or four persons who know Veda-s in entirety. Even if a thousand people who do not know Veda-s say, it will not become dharma.' None will argue that Mahāperiyavā was among those few who lived the Veda-s, and his every word is Veda vākyam.

Although it is not easy for an ordinary person to interpret the words of enlightened masters, I am hereby making a tiny attempt to

---

3 चत्वारो वा त्रयो वापि यं ब्रूयुर्वेदपारगाः सधर्मेति विज्ञेयो नेतरैस्तु सहस्रशः ७

  Parāśara Smṛti (Chapter 8, verse 7)

share the deep scientific insights contained in the rules of the śāstra, as spoken by Mahāperiyavā, and as revealed to me through the blessings of Guru-s and Devī's anugraha. May this scribe be forgiven for any errors in understanding arising out of her own limitations in accessing the realm of jñānaṃ in its entirety.

A Note to The Reader

Nothing can truly be comprehended without direct experience. Those spiritual seekers who have had experiences of the subtle realm will easily relate to what is given in this book. For others, attempting to understand the subtle nuances behind injunctions in the śāstra-s might not happen without a few hits and misses and maybe even injuries in the process. For those who are aware that they have broken the rules in the śāstra in their own life, journeying through this book might, at times, feel like entering uncertain dark tunnels. The darkness is only because of one's own guilt and resistance in finding the truth. If that happens, it might help to remember that the only way out of the tunnel is to make the whole journey to the other end, where the light is.

Reading this book should be done with a sincere intention to seek the truth for one's own spiritual progress. Setting aside thoughts of proving a point or looking for means to respond to criticism of caste narratives, this book is best absorbed when one seeks in a state of inner silence for the only reason to know the truth for oneself.

There is no doubt that those dharmic organisations who have broken the rules in the śāstra-s have done so out of kindness towards women and the śūdra varṇa and with the loving intention of promoting what is considered equality through the Western lens. Doing things when ignorant but with good intentions is understandable. But once the light has dawned, refraining from changing will be an impediment to one's own spiritual journey, even if we disregard the injury it causes to others. May this book help such organisations make the right decisions for their own welfare and that of those whom they guide.

As for the women (and others) who may have broken the rules in search of a spiritual path - you have already borne the consequences of taking a path that was not meant for you and suffered enough. Be kind to yourself and gather the courage to know the truth, which alone can set you free.

If this book has come to you, it is for a reason. Trust that, and proceed with the curiosity and honesty of a true seeker. Be assured that there is light at the end of the tunnel, so make sure you make it to the end.

Introduction

One of the thousand names of Devī in the Lalitā Sahasranāma is वर्णाश्रम-विधायिनी (Varṇāśrama-vidhāyinī) (no.286), which means, She who has established the system of the varṇa-s and aśrama-s.[4] In other verses, Devī is referred to as मातृकावर्णरूपिणी (mātṛka varṇa rūpiṇī) (no.577) which means, She who is in the form of the letters of the alphabet, and again She is referred to as वर्णरूपिणी (varṇa rūpiṇī) (no.850), meaning the personification of the letters of the alphabets.

Devī upāsak-s will understand that when a quality is attributed to Devī, it is an indication that it is not a man-made social construct. In the context of understanding varṇa, when Devī is referred to as varṇāśrama vidhāyinī or varṇa rūpiṇī, it means that varṇa is a biological quality that is inherent in the physical body when an ātma takes a human form. Therefore, this book is an exploration of the biological basis of varṇa dharma.

Meaning of varṇa

A few years ago, a kind friend signed me up for a short online 'Saṃskṛtam Appreciation' course.[5] On the very first day of the course, the teacher, Dr. Sampadananda Mishra ji, said something I could never forget. He began by saying that in Saṃskṛtam, every word is

---

4 Aśrama refers to the four stages of life - brahmacārya, gṛhasthāśrama, vānaprasthāśrama and sanyāsa. These will not be discussed in this book.

5 This course was organized by City Book Leaders, an online platform for book lovers.

actually revealed to seers and not a product of man's intellect. He said that each word is conscious of its own history and has a root sound and that root sounds are connected with experiences. He then said that Saṃskṛtam can only be understood through contemplation. By meditation upon each word, he said that the word will reveal itself. He also suggested doing the upāsana of this language as a śakti.

It was the most phenomenal thing to be said about a language and naturally seems too abstract to be true. And yet, that is how the meaning of the word varṇa was revealed in this book. It is true that there are several layers of understanding for every word in Saṃskṛtam, and therefore, what is shared in this book is probably just one layer deeper than the popular narrative. But if it has occurred to me, certainly such a meaning would have occurred to others as well. After all, as Sampad ji said, thoughts, once formed, do not disappear; they remain in the ākāśa tattva. So, it should be possible that whoever tunes in to the ākāśa tattva in contemplation of the word varṇa, will receive the deeper meaning, whether or not they read this book.

Sometimes, such revelations happen even without a conscious effort, as it happened in the case of this book, through the means of listening to Devī's thousand names. Those who regularly listen to the Lalitā Sahasranāma might notice that every once in a while, a particular name will repeatedly play in the mind without our consciously seeking it. During one such time, the name *varṇāśrama vidhāyinī* happened. When Devī Herself brings our attention to something, all we need to do is be with that, and She will communicate what it means. Thus, a thought was planted that we need to look into the most common meaning of varṇa, which is colour, and that varṇa dharma has something to do with colour. Later, it also occurred that the word varṇa is used to denote syllabic or lettered speech, known as varṇātmaka śabda.[6] Thus, we have varṇa as colour and varṇa as sound.

---

6 Note that Varṇātmaka śabda is different from unlettered sound or dhvani known as Dhvanyātmaka śabda.

But how could colour or sound create a four-fold division of humankind? Certainly, colour here does not mean skin colour. We humans are many more shades of brown, black and white than just four. So, colour of what, then? And what does sound have to do with it? This is what we shall explore in this book - varṇa, the four-fold division of humans, as a result of inherent, but subtle, colour and sound capability.

Why this, now?

It must be mentioned that studying or writing about varṇa dharma as a separate subject was not part of the initial plan. After all, there are several trust-worthy Indic scholars in recent times who have logically and successfully dismissed the colonial narrative of caste and brought in the understanding of varṇa based on jāti (occupation), guṇa (characteristic) and karma (action). It is their excellent and tireless work that allows this book the luxury of taking the understanding of varṇa to a deeper level. Therefore, it is only right that we begin by expressing sincere and heartfelt gratitude to all those whose work has spared us the necessity to start from scratch by dismissing the colonial caste narrative.

A question might arise: if the existing work on varṇa based on jāti, guṇa and karma is not wrong, then what is the need for this book?

The current understanding of varṇa based on jāti, guṇa and karma is not incorrect; it is just incomplete. While the jāti-guṇa-karma-based understanding satisfies most of the common concerns about the social order and social structure of Bhārat's past, it struggles to explain specific rules pertaining to women (of menstrual age) and the śūdra varṇa, both of whom are often categorised together in several instances (e.g., eligibility for upanayana, Vedic mantra chanting, agni kriyā, etc.).

For anyone concerned about the health and well-being of women and the śūdra varṇa, finding answers that explain the rules as given in the śāstra-s becomes necessary, not only because several people are asking questions regarding these rules but also because of the increasing practice of teaching Vedic mantra-s, yajña-s and advanced yoga kriyā to those for whom such methods were traditionally never prescribed. Further, demands from activists to change the current law, which does not allow women and the śūdra varṇa to officiate as arcaka-s (priests) in temples where brāhmaṇa men are arcaka-s, is causing this issue to be taken up in the courts from the rights-based standpoint. States like Tamil Nadu[7] and Kerala[8] have already had to make changes and pass bills that now allow women[9] and men of all varṇa-s to have the 'right' to be trained and to officiate as temple arcaka-s. While this might seem like social progress, we need to ask why this was not recommended by the dharmaśāstra texts, which are based on the Veda-s and, therefore, have only that in mind which is the highest good for all members of society. Equally important is the need to contemplate how breaking these age-old truths declared in the śāstra might biologically affect women and the śūdra varṇa, in whose name these rules are being broken.

Methodology

In writing this book, there has been an attempt, although unstructured, to apply the scientific methodology and guidelines proposed by the Ṣaṭ Darśana, which are considered the foremost among the ancient Bhāratiya texts that developed the rational and logical system of arriving at the truth. For example, the scientific methodology as per the Vaiśeṣika Darśana prescribes the following

---

7 Article: Non-Brahmin priests in Tamil Nadu: A progressive step. Deccan Herald. 22 October 2021

8 Article: In A First, Non-Brahmins & Dalits To Be Appointed As Priests In Kerala. Homegrown.co.in., 08 Jun 2021

9 Article: Tamil Nadu Govt Appoints 3 Women Priests In Hindu Temples, CM MK Stalin 'Hails New Era Of Inclusivity And Equality.' Outlook India. 15 Sep 2023

steps - uddeśa (proposition or enumeration of the subject matter), the ascertainment of essential characteristics or marks (the pramāṇa-s) by definitions (lakṣaṇa) and descriptions (upalakṣaṇa), examination (parīkṣā) and verification (nirṇaya).[10]

In the Bhāratiya Jñāna Parampara, now also known as the Indian Knowledge Systems (IKS), we use pramāṇa-s as the proof of knowledge. This serves as one of the core concepts in Indian epistemology[11] and is considered a valid means of arriving at the truth. While the Saṅkhyā, Yog, Nyāya, Vaiśeṣika Darśana as well as Āyurveda primarily use the four pramāṇa-s, namely, pratyakṣa (direct perception), anumāna (inference), upamāna (comparison) and śabda (valid testimony such as from the Vedas), there is also arthāpatti (postulation, presumption) and anupalabdi (non-perception, cognitive proof using non-existence) as per Advaita Vedānta. The reason for listing these pramāṇa-s is that even if readers disagree with what is written in this book, they can proceed in their own way using this framework of arriving at the truth as per the IKS. A simplified explanation of each pramāṇa is provided below for those who might not be familiar with it.

    i. Pratyakṣa: this refers to cognition through direct perception. The knowledge gained through this method could be of two types. The first type is savikalpa pratyakṣa pramāṇa, obtained when the five senses (ears, eyes, tongue, nose, skin) come in contact with an object or situation. The second type is nirvikalpa pratyakṣa pramāṇa, which is the knowledge perceived beyond the senses when the mind comes in contact with the ātma. For pratyakṣa pramāṇa to be free of falsehood, it is necessary for the sense organs and mental faculties to be

---

10 Seal, Brajendranath. The Positive Sciences of the Ancient Hindus, 1915

11 Epistemology is the means of acquiring knowledge, especially with regard to its methods, validity, and scope, and the distinction between justified belief and opinion.

in sound health and for the perceiver's mind to be free from egoistic or passion-caused agitations.

ii. Anumāna: This refers to knowledge gained about a particular object/situation by knowing another object/situation. Typically, anumāna is referred to as knowledge gained through inference. Anumāna can be used to validate or re-affirm knowledge gained through pratyakṣa pramāṇa.

iii. Upamāna: This refers to knowledge obtained by comparing an unknown object to a known object that is similar. Typically, upamāna is referred to as the proof obtained through similarities or analogy.

iv. Śabda: This refers to knowledge obtained from a valid/authoritative source such as the Veda-s. It is also called śruti pramāṇa, āgama pramāṇa or āptavacana. Often, when humans fail to perceive things through the sense organs, we can rely only on the knowledge gained by the ṛṣi-s who knew how to access the realm of the source of all knowledge through their experience of samādhi. The Veda-s and all the texts based on the Veda-s, such as the smṛti, purāṇa, āgama śāstra and tantra texts, are the product of such knowledge. If there is uncertainty about any principle even though pratyakṣa, anumāna and upamāna have been used to reason, then śabda pramāṇa can be considered as the means of removing the confusion. While the first three methods use the human intellectual experience and reasoning capacity, śabda pramāṇa is derived from the deeper level that delves into the source of wisdom in a state devoid of ego and hence should be considered irrefutable.

v. Arthāpatti: This is a method used to remove inconsistencies between the presented knowledge and the facts. It is the presumption of something from the explanation of a known fact. It can be used when a perceived fact cannot be explained without some other fact. In such cases, one can presuppose or postulate the existence of this other fact even though it is not perceived. Arthāpatti pramāṇa can be an important tool to explain exceptions and seeming contradictions in understanding.

vi. Anupalabdi: This is a means of knowledge through cognition of non-existence. Here, negation is considered as a means of valid knowledge.

Applying the above framework to our context, this book has the following structure:

1. Purpose (uddeśa): To arrive at the reason for the difference in rules for women and the śūdra varṇa in comparison to the other varṇa-s, according to the rules prescribed in the dharmaśāstra texts. This uddeśa has been covered in this very chapter titled 'Introduction.'

2. Lakṣaṇa & Upalakṣaṇa: This has been covered in the following sections, which explore the biological basis of varṇa dharma based on the following pramāṇa-s:

   i. Pratyakṣa pramāṇa: First-hand knowledge obtained as a result of the direct experiences of women. This has been covered in the first chapter titled 'Experiences of women.'

   ii. Śabda pramāṇa: The textual evidence for the difference in rules for women and the śūdra varṇa. This has primarily been covered in the second chapter titled 'Dharmaśāstra rules.' Overall, more than a hundred saṃskṛtam references from various ancient texts have been provided throughout the book as śabda pramāṇa for the conclusions drawn.

   iii. Anumāna & Upamāna: The third, fourth, fifth and sixth chapters titled 'Varṇa as Colour', 'Varṇa as Sound', 'Upanayana Saṃskāra' and 'Agnikriyā' respectively, use the methods of anumāna and upamāna to explore the inference we can arrive at from the pratyakṣa pramāṇa stated as well as from the śabda pramāṇa. The third chapter includes the Puruṣa Sūkta definition of varṇa as emerging from different parts of the body of the Supreme Puruṣa as mentioned in the ṚgVeda, the guṇa-karma based definition of varṇa from chapter eighteen of the Bhagvad Gītā and Śrīmad Bhāgavatam, as well as the understanding from some of the yogōpaniṣad texts and tantra. References and citations from modern published studies are also included wherever possible.

    iv. Arthāpatti (postulation, presumption): This method has been used to explore the reasons for the cases of exceptions such as the purāṇa based references of women & persons of the śūdra varṇa who had siddhi-s and seeming contradictions to the śāstra rules such as that of brahmavādini-s, ṛṣika-s and yoginī-s. This will be covered in the sixth chapter titled 'Exceptions.'

    v. Anupalabdi: This method shall be used to put together evidence of non-mentioning of women and śūdra varṇa in the dharmaśāstra texts as valid proof that these practices were not meant for women. This has been included in the section on śabda pramāṇa in chapter two, which lists the rules as per the dharmaśāstra texts.

3. Nirṇaya: Concluding findings, which will be covered in the final chapter titled 'Conclusion.'

Those who are familiar with formal research studies will observe that many of the steps outlined by this system are quite similar to what is proposed by modern science's research methodology. What is different in the case of this book is the absence of quantitative data.[12] The use of quantitative data becomes important if a study

---

12 Quantitative data refers to the systematic empirical investigation of observable phenomena via statistical, mathematical, or computational techniques.

is attempting to establish a new fact. Whereas, in this work, we are only re-establishing the validity of existing rules for women and the śūdra varṇa as per the śāstra-s, which have either been forgotten or have not been taken seriously due to lack of satisfactory reasoning suitable to our times. To do this, we will utilise the elaborate way of reasoning through pramāṇa-s, which stress the epistemological ways of knowing, thereby making it possible even for a layperson to have a framework within which to reason and arrive at conclusions.

For those who are comfortable with the IKS, the above process of arriving at the understanding of the biological basis of varṇa should suffice. However, there will be many instances where concepts are explained through the language of Western science as well, to make it easier for those who are more familiar with Western scientific language. Thus, you will find that there are modern scientific theories and published research papers to provide evidence of what is stated in the śāstra-s. Science, after all, is one; what varies is the depth of understanding.

Chapter 1: Experiences Of Women

Among the many stories received from women after Ṛtu Vidyā,[13] those which resulted in this book are lessons learnt from personal stories of rebellion, of breaking traditional rules prescribed for women, and of suffering as a consequence. Women shared stories of how visiting certain Śiva temples and mokṣa dhām-s, even though they were not menstruating at the time of the visit, messed up their menstrual cycles; how meditation for long duration focusing on the ājña cakra (between eyebrows) led to menstrual disorders; how intense hatha yoga training had stopped menstruation for months; how yoga aimed at raising the kuṇḍalinī had disrupted their family life along with causing menstrual problems; how regular chanting of Vedic mantra-s had made the menstrual cycle unpredictable and painful; how performing agnikriyā (fire rituals) themselves affected menstrual patterns; how initiation into certain esoteric religious practices which were typically forbidden for women, made it difficult to conceive, and so on.

While Ṛtu Vidyā provided answers to what women should not do at the time of menstruation and the biological reason for it, it did not go into the details of the rules for women pursuing the ādhyātmika mārg (spiritual path). The repeated question asked by several women was: 'If these spiritual practices cannot be done by us, what then is prescribed (as per the śāstra-s) as the sādhanā mārg for women of menstrual age?'

---

13 "Ṛtu Vidyā: Ancient science behind menstrual practices", is a book published by the same author in the year 2020. It provides explanations of the science behind traditional menstrual practices.

It was in search of answers to this question that the next book, which is an interpretation of the Strī Dharma Paddhati,[14] began to take shape. But that work became difficult because of the repeated mention of rules for women citing varṇa dharma. In many instances, such as for upanayana (sacred thread ceremony), śaucācāra (hygienic practices), ācamana (ritual sipping of water) and even for snāna (bathing), there is a similar set of rules for women and the śūdra varṇa, which are different from what is prescribed for the other three varṇa-s. In order to comprehend the rules for women, it became necessary to comprehend varṇa dharma as a whole, and especially the rules for the śūdra varṇa, given that women were often put in the same category as the śūdra varṇa. The initial thought of adding the explanation for varṇa dharma as a small chapter in the work on Strī Dharma Paddhati became laughable as the depth of understanding required to even scratch the surface of this concept became clearer, necessitating this work to become a separate book. Therefore, this book on the biological basis of varṇa dharma is specifically intended to be able to comprehend the varṇa rules for women of menstrual age and the śūdra varṇa, although it might answer many other questions pertaining to varṇa dharma as a whole, as an unintended consequence.

Consequences of breaking the rules

Any girl/woman of menstrual age who has been made to chant Vedic mantra-s or perform agnikriyā-s as prescribed in the Vedic karma kāṇḍa for six months or more has a high probability of experiencing problematic menstruation. Only six months is mentioned because that is how long it might take for one to recognise that there is a problem. The problem itself would have started much earlier, and

---

14 Strīdharmapaddhati is an 18th-century Saṃskṛtam text written by the court pandit Tryambakayajvan in the Thanjavur Maratha kingdom. It is a compilation of existing rules from dharmaśāstra texts and purāṇa-s, specifically for women.

those who can tune in to experience subtle phenomena will know it from the start.

The menstrual disturbance typically starts with the menstrual cycle becoming unpredictable and irregular, which is often ignored as a minor problem. Menstrual health is closely connected to mental and emotional health. So, when the cycle becomes unpredictable, the earliest experiences could be emotional turmoil, playing out as stress and mood swings. When ignored, it could manifest in a more severe way through the experience of period pain, excessive bleeding or the other extreme of very scanty flow. When ignored for long periods of time while continuing to do what is forbidden by the śāstra-s, women could develop menstrual disorders such as ovarian dysfunction (including PCOD), inversed menstrual flow such as endometriosis, hyperandrogenism (developing masculine qualities such as facial hair, rough voice, aggressive personality) due to excessive testosterone, and other complications. Many of them are likely to face difficulty while attempting to conceive, or if they manage to conceive, then labour and delivery may involve complications. Sometimes, the problem becomes so severe and irreversible that a hysterectomy (removal of the uterus) is recommended by gynaecologists.[15] If they somehow escape such a fate, early menopause can be expected if they continue the chanting of Vedic mantra-s or undertake other practices which are prohibited as per the śāstra-s.

If these are the complications on the physical front, there are significant changes that occur emotionally and mentally as well. A repulsion or indifference towards saṃsāra (worldly life and responsibilities) and a vairāgya bhāva (sense of detachment)

---

15 According to Āyurveda, the uterus is considered as a woman's second heart, and plays an important role in Vāta regulation, absorption of calcium and prevention of bone-related issues even after menopause. Therefore, removal of the uterus is rarely suggested in Āyurveda, while the focus is on preventing menstrual disorders through the several rules and regulations for women of menstrual age.

from worldly duties are experienced by some. As a result, young unmarried women might not prefer to enter into matrimony and may choose the life of a brahmacārini. For one who is born with a female form, this is an unnatural (against nature's way) state of being. Women's bodies are created with the possibility of experiencing bhukti (worldly pursuits) while creating and nurturing life during menstrual years and mukti (spiritual liberation) after menopause if the rules of the śāstra are followed. However, due to the lack of understanding of how these rules impact women's biology, we continue to break the rules and put women through dire consequences, which are very much avoidable.

On a subtler level, those women who have been trained in specialised yoga practices such as kriya yoga, hatha yoga, or chant mantra-s which are specifically meant to raise the kuṇḍalini and activate the pineal gland, might experience an additional set of issues. These are advanced practices that connect the practitioner to other realms and dimensions. If the individual's body and mind are not designed to handle such experiences, it can have severe psychological effects and cause disturbed mental states, in addition to having an impaired menstrual cycle. Examples of this are shared later in this book.

Pratyakṣa pramāṇa: Direct experiences of women

To help us ground the narrative in real experiences and serve as the pratyakṣa pramāṇa for this topic, a few personal incidents are shared below in some detail, without mentioning any names to protect the identity of those who shared.

Śiva temples and mokṣa dhām-s

An important incident happened at the Śrī Vaikom Mahadeva (Śiva) temple in Kerala to a female devotee. On the day of the visit, an elaborate abhiṣeka had just begun, and the vibrations in the temple were perceptibly high. Standing close to the sanctum during the abhiṣeka and pūjā that followed for around 30–40 minutes made her a little lightheaded, and she felt the need to sit down. She barely sat for about 10 or 15 minutes when she slipped into a deep meditative state effortlessly. During those few short moments, there was also a clear vision that appeared. As soon as she stepped out of the temple precincts, her menstrual period began unexpectedly, a week before its predicted date. The first two days of this period had unusually scanty flow, and the entire body experienced reverberations like a plucked string instrument. This experience triggered a similar set of experiences that entire year, with meditation even at home leading to visions, followed by a sudden start of menstruation before its scheduled time. These incidents happened especially on special occasions like Navarātri or Śivarātri where the energy was naturally conducive for meditation, and even the slightest effort had such outcomes. Needless to say, the frequent changes in the menstrual cycle created quite a disturbance in her physical and emotional health. It took about a year's effort to consciously avoid certain practices before her menstrual cycle returned to normalcy.

Interestingly, the Vaikom Mahadeva temple is not only known as one of the most powerful Śiva temples of Kerala, but it is also famous as the site of satyagraha where Mahatma Gandhi and Periyar led a movement to abolish what they called 'untouchability and caste-discrimination.'[16] Back in the day, this temple's rules did not encourage people of the śūdra varṇa to enter the premises. Contemplating the above experience, it seems like a direct insight into the reason for the traditional rule. While women's bodies respond to such states by inducing menstruation through the downward flow of apāna to balance the sudden upward surge of

---

16 Ranjani, Lalitha: Remembering Vaikom Satyagraha: A movement that spearheaded social reforms in two States

prāṇa,[17] if this happened to the body of a śūdra man, there might not be an external obvious sign such as menstruation. However, the external signs experienced are only a manifestation of something more happening internally at a subtle level, which we shall explore in greater detail in the other chapters of this book.

It might be important for readers to know that similar experiences have happened to other women who visited Śiva temples known as 'powerful',[18] even though they did not sit in meditation. The following incidents are first-hand accounts of what the women have shared with the author. One incident was of an American woman who got her period unexpectedly soon after stepping out after visiting the Mahākāla temple in Nepal. A similar incident is recorded in the book Ṛtu Vidyā of a woman whose period unexpectedly started while at the Kapāleśwar temple in Chennai, how she temporarily lost consciousness and how her instincts urged her to leave the temple immediately. The other incident is of a woman whose period started unexpectedly while at a Śiva temple in Śrisailam; she was unable to step out immediately, due to which her cycle became problematic ever since the visit. Yet another incident is of a woman who did a rudrābhiṣeka at the Kashi Vishwanath temple and whose period after the visit was unusually painful. And then there are the personal testimonials of at least five other women who visited Śiva temples, which are part of mokṣa dhām-s and tīrtha yatra-s, namely Jageshwar Dham, Kedarnath, Badrinath and the Kailash-Manasarovar yatra. In

---

17 Apāna is one of the pañca prāṇa-s (five forms of prāṇa) in the body, which governs functions necessitating downward movement in the body, such as urination, defecation, menstruation, child birth, etc. While prāṇa (another of the pañca prāṇa) moves upwards, apāna moves downwards, and the balance between the two is what keeps humans healthy and alive.

18 When a Śiva temple is colloquially referred to as 'powerful', it means that people experience a high vibration state in such a space, without much effort. Other temples of Śiva, where he is in a milder form, or as a gṛhastha (householder) along with Devī, such as Sundareshwar in the Madurai Meenakshi temple, is unlikely to have such an impact.

these cases, their period started unexpectedly, before time, and in a couple of women, it resulted in complications that lasted for years.

Like the Vaikom temple's traditional rules, mokṣa dhām-s were never meant for women of menstrual age or for people who are deeply involved in saṃsāra. Hindu-s will recollect how a few generations ago, it was only grandparents who would go on such tīrtha yātra-s after they had completed most of their worldly responsibilities and there was a natural desire for mokṣa.[19] It didn't have to be spelt out as a rule, as it was commonly known and understood that such places are not for women of menstrual age or for those who aren't yet ready.

An incident that happened in a village in Karnataka where we were working gives us some important clues. During one of our visits to this village in the year 2018–19, the local leader, who happened to be of a brāhmaṇa varṇa, took us to the temple he had built. He told us that in spite of several invitations and requests to the people in the scheduled caste (SC) and scheduled tribe (ST) colonies, who live in the lane adjacent to the temple, they refused to enter the temple. The brāhmaṇa man requested us to talk to the SC/ST people and convince them to enter the temple, which he insisted was built for everyone in the village. So, the SC/ST people were called, and we asked them why they refused to enter the temple. After some hesitation in talking to strangers, they told us that if they entered the temple of brāhmaṇa-s,[20]

---

19 A simplified explanation of Mokṣa Dhām-s is that these are places that facilitate the ātma to leave the physical body through the upper apertures by raising prāṇa upwards. By its nature, such places are life-negating and are not meant for those who are biologically in the reproductive phase of life and/or have a desire for worldly pursuits.

20 The temples that the SC/ST people typically prefer are temples of grāma devatā-s, which are village deities, mostly in ugra rūpa (fierce form). These temples correspond to the lower cakra-s which are necessary for doing physical work and for maintaining robustness of health required for hard physical work. In contrast, temples built by brāhmaṇa-s are more to do with the higher cakra-s that aid intellectual work & higher knowledge. It is

they would not be able to do their day-to-day work properly. The SC/ST people said nothing about caste oppression or fear of the upper-class brāhmaṇa and all the other cooked-up reasons that the popular narrative has been feeding us with. Instead, they said something very tangible, very biological, and so unpretentiously, as though it should have been obvious.

This incident was an eye-opener and made us wonder if the truth behind the 'untouchability and caste-discrimination' narratives might be completely the opposite of what has been portrayed. It is highly likely that the so-called oppressed people themselves, with full awareness of consequences arising out of the experience, chose not to enter certain spaces. Having come across such opposite narratives around menstrual practices, which have been documented in Ṛtu Vidyā, it makes it easier to understand that the truth might indeed be more biological than social.

Vedic mantra chanting

The other incident that might be important to share is an experience that happened at an event organised by an educational institute. The institution was part of a religious organisation in the name of a well-known saint of recent times. The place also had a Vedic gurukul where regular chanting of the Veda-s was done by the students. As a result, the place had high vibrations owing to the regular chanting, and anyone who could perceive subtle phenomena could have easily experienced it.

I was invited to deliver a talk to the college-going students as part of an event they had organised. On this campus, they were teaching

---

highly likely that the villagers in the SC/ST colonies knew by experience that temples of grāma devatā-s help them in their day-to-day physical work, whereas temples of brāhmaṇa-s come in the way of their work and lifestyle. For more information on temples and cakra-s, refer the book 'Women and Sabarimala' written by the same author.

the Vedic mantra-s to teenage girls as well, and I naturally wondered if their menstrual cycle might not have been affected as a result of chanting. As I began delivering the talk based on Ṛtu Vidyā and paused for questions, I did not have to wonder for long, as the girls themselves shared that they often experience severe period pain and irregularity and are only now beginning to recognise the reason for it. Some of them even sent emails after the event, asking what could be done to repair their disrupted cycle. Typically, we would think that for girls who live a sattvic lifestyle, eat healthy, practice yoga, chant Vedic mantra-s, and live on a peaceful campus, their menstrual experience should have been anything but painful, but that was not the case. This is a clear pointer that the gurukul-based Vedic learning was traditionally not for girls for reasons that are biological, as will be explained later in this book.

Since then, I have heard similar experiences of disturbed menstrual cycles from other young girls from modern gurukuls where they are being taught Vedic mantra-s. On the few occasions where I have attempted to intervene and suggest alternative ways, the management became uncomfortable, making me step back and let it go. As organisations get bigger, admitting mistakes and changing the track becomes very difficult.

Women officiating in temple-s

Given below is the first-hand narrative of a young brahmacārini associated with a spiritual organisation who was asked to undertake certain rituals in a temple outside Bhārat when the traditional arcaka-s from Bhārat could not continue owing to COVID restrictions. She comes from a Śrī Vaiṣṇava Viśiṣṭa Advaita Brāhmaṇa family, and the organisation she served follows the Advaita Sampradāya. This was shared by the narrator via email to me.

"I was the primary caretaker for a temple with pratiṣṭhāpita mūrti-s of Meenākṣi Amma, Soma Sundareśwara, Śrī Ganapati and Śrī Kṛṣṇa. Though we had a trained arcaka initially, due to COVID restrictions, they were not able to continue and returned to Bhārat. There were sevak-s to complete the Sundareśwara and Śrī Kṛṣṇa weekly abhiṣekam-s. Nitya pūjā was divided among the sevak-s and myself. The Devī abhiṣekam seva primarily fell on myself and another sevak (both biological menstruating-age females). We did have another male sevak come support from time to time. We offered abhiṣekam to Devī twice a month from March 2021 to March 2022. I did not do the abhiṣekam seva during my menstruation but I was pushed to help with alaṅkāra. Devī's mūrti is over 5 feet tall and she stands on a 2-foot pīṭham. The mūrti is solid granite and was sculpted in Tamil Nadu and pratiṣṭhāpana was done in June 2014.

The first few months that I began conducting the abhiṣekam-s, my menstrual cycle started to get more painful and my energy levels were sinking fast. Both anxiety and stress started increasing. The energies in the temple were hanging by a thread. By the summer of 2021, my fatigue prevented me from conducting even my regular sādhanā and I struggled severely with my mental and physical health. Though Devī allowed us to celebrate Navarātri 2021, on dhasara day I struggled to get out of my bed due to the intense fatigue and had to be escorted home after the abhiṣekam. I took bed rest for a week. By this time my menstrual cycle was entirely tampered with and unsettled. My responsibilities to the temple pushed me to continue with the nitya pūjā-s and abhiṣekam-s even though I knew it was affecting myself and the temple poorly. In March 2022, I met with a catastrophic car accident and the doctors stated that I should have been dead or severely paralysed. I was chanting a Devī bhajan during the crash and I believe that was the only reason I was saved. Devī took care of me and ensured that I took bed rest for 6 weeks. By Guru and Bhagavān's grace, the COVID Visa hold/backup had subsided by then and we were able to have two highly and traditionally trained arcaka-s (both biological male) from Bhārat join our temple and revitalise the environment.

We were quarantined for the year and only opened to the public starting Śivarātri 2022. We were looking forward to the chanting of Ekādaśa Rudra to re-energise the temple. Our new arcaka-s came in April 2022 and as a part of our Temple Anniversary Utsava in June 2022 we conducted a puṇyāhavācanam and intense pārāyaṇaṃ by the arcaka-s.

While we (females) did the abhiṣekam seva, we were not able to chant and do the seva so the dravya-s were not energised to the maximum as they should be. Therefore, the caitanya emanating from the mūrti decreased and was felt in the sannidhi and could be seen in the reduced prakāśa in Devī's face. When the arcaka-s (males) came, they not only established śuddhi through pārāyaṇaṃ and subsequently the puṇyāhavācanam, they also were able to use more dravya-s and energise them through the specific mantra-s per dravya and offer it to Devī. When Devī's darśan was given after the alaṅkāra, during the nīrājanam it felt as though a Divya Jyoti had returned to her Divya mukha. Also, when the arcaka-s chanted their kṣamā prārthanā, we were all enveloped by the love, compassion, and forgiveness in the sannidhi. Just as a mother is, this Jaganmatha disciplines us strictly when needed and showers us with unconditional love when we realise and seek forgiveness for our shortcomings."

This honest personal experience gives us much to contemplate and will be discussed in chapter four. The experiences that have been shared here are just a few of the hundreds of emails received after Ṛtu Vidyā. If these experiences were one-off incidents that happened to a few women here and there, it could have been considered a mere coincidence. But when we realise that these incidents are occurring in the cases where the śāstra-s specifically prohibit these practices, then we need to sit up and take notice. The incidents shared by women and my own experiences gave me an idea of what could happen when the body of a woman of menstrual age goes into states of high vibration. This is important to understand because all the prohibited rules as per the śāstra-s pertain to those practices or places that cause the body to vibrate at a higher frequency than what is the natural state for the person to whom the rule applies. These rules are anything but discriminatory and are put in place as a preventive and protective measure for those whose physical bodies cannot handle vibrations higher than their natural capacity.[21]

---

21 In the chapters that follow, there will be details provided of what is technically meant by 'high vibrations.'

Chapter 2: Dharmaśāstra Rules

What is the Dharma Śāstra?

Every Hindu is aware that there are four goals of life for a mortal human: dharma, artha, kāma and mokṣa. Rightly understood, this means that when the pursuit of even artha and kāma is done as per dharma, that too will lead towards mokṣa. Kalidasa said, 'Śarīramādyaṃ khalu dharmasādhanam',[22] meaning that the human body is the vehicle for one to work in dharma (towards the goal of mokṣa). It is said that even the demigods and other celestial beings need to take birth in human form in order to obtain a body with which they can attain mokṣa. But the moment the ātma enters a human body at birth, the illusion called māya takes over, and the being forgets all its previous births and lessons learnt. It may have been a highly learned scholar in its previous birth but now remembers nothing and starts from scratch as a very ordinary mortal in a new place and sometimes in a different age. When such is the case, what can help this lost ātma find its way back and continue the journey towards mokṣa from where it left off in its previous birth? That help is obtained from the rules, which we call Dharma Śāstra. The word śāstra, in many Indian languages, is the word used for science. What science? That science, by living which, the ātma can continue its journey in dharma in every birth, without wasting time wandering around trying to find its purpose. Dharmaśāstra texts provide the shortest possible path to mokṣa, for all of us who identify with the body.

---

22 शरीरमाद्यं खलु धर्मसाधनम् | Kālidāsa in Kumārasambhavam [5.33]

In other words, the rules that govern the body to enable it to work towards mokṣa, even while pursuing artha and kāma, are the rules in the smṛti texts, which we call the Dharmaśāstra. These texts comprise rules for Vedic rituals (śrauta dharma); then, there is the set of rules for non-ritualistic day-to-day living, which come under the varnāśrama dharma (smārta dharma). Unknown to many Hindu-s of today is an interesting fact about the very definition of who we call a Hindu. In the words of Mahāperiyavā:

> "At the times of Ādi Śankarācārya, those who belonged to the Sanātana Dharma Vedic religion were called smārta-s, which simply meant followers of the smṛti-s. Smṛti meant Dharma Śāstra."

So, Dharmaśāstra lies at the very core of considering oneself a Hindu, and the rules contained in it provide the means to work towards mokṣa, using the physical body as a vehicle for this accomplishment.

What are the texts that come under Dharmaśāstra?

Broadly speaking, Dharmaśāstra contains instructions regarding religious duty, ceremonies, legal duty and more. The smṛti texts which are derived from the Veda-s, and presented in the form of a code of law (ex. Manu smṛti, Yājñavalkya smṛti, Gautama Dharmasūtra, Parāśara smṛti, etc.), are the main sources of the dharmaśāstra. There are also the rules for domestic ceremonies known as saṃskāra-s in the form of the Gṛhya Sūtra-s, derived again from the Veda-s (śruti) and smṛti-s, which are specific to those belonging to a particular sampradāya (tradition) within the Vedic religion. For example, Āpastamba Gṛhya Sūtra is relevant for those who follow Krishna Yajur Veda, whereas Gobhila Gṛhya Sūtra is relevant for those who follow Sāma Veda, and so on.[23]

---

23 The different Gṛhya Sutra texts for each Veda, can be referred at this link - https://greenmesg.org/bharatavarsha/scriptures/Vedangas/grihya_sutras.php

Each sampradāya and further divisions within it are indicative of a highly customised set of rules that apply to specific genetic traits in individuals from that sub-set. This is to be kept in mind because scholars often quote the gṛhya sūtra rules as a generic rule for all Hindu-s, creating quite a bit of confusion. What applies to one sampradāya need not apply to another, and therefore, each rule from the gṛhya sūtra, if quoted or referred, must be examined in the context of the sampradāya to which it belongs.

Regarding the smṛti texts, Manu Smṛti is the foremost text which cannot be ignored. Manu is said to have the highest authority among smṛti-s and that smṛti which is opposed to the dicta of Manu is not commended. This is expressed as given below:

वेदार्थोपनिबन्द्धृत्वात्प्राधान्यं तु मनुस्मृतौ ।

मन्वर्थविपरीता या स्मृतिः सा न प्रशस्यते ।।[24]

While Parāśara smṛti[25] is said to be the relevant text for our times, that is, for Kali-yuga, it does not differ from Manu in most of the rules that will be covered in this book. The main difference in Parāśara smṛti for our context is the slight flexibility in terms of the occupations that each of the dvija-s[26] can undertake owing to it being Kali-yuga. However, the rules for women and the śūdra varṇa, which will be explored in this book, are similar in the majority of the smṛti texts.

---

24 Vide 'History of Dharmaśāstra' by Dr. P.V. Kane, Volume II, Part 1, Chapter IX, Page 465. Here it is mentioned that it is by बृहस्पति Bṛhaspati quoted by अपरार्क Aparārka on Yājñavalkya II.21 and कुल्लूक (Kulluka) on Manu I.1.

25 Parāśara Smṛti (Chapter 1, verse 24) - कृते तु मानवा धर्मास्त्रेतायाम गौतमाः स्मृताः द्वापरे शाङ्खलिखिताः कलौ पाराशराः स्मृताः २४. 'For Kṛta (yuga), are suited the laws of Manu, for the Tretā the laws of Gautama, for Dvāpara those by Shank and Likhita, and for Kali, the laws by Parāśara are prescribed.'

26 Dvija (twice-born men) is a term used to indicate those who have had the upanayana ceremony and includes men from the brāhmaṇa, kṣatriya and vaiśya varṇa

Are Veda and śāstra different?

Some scholars might think that the Veda-s are more reliable than the śāstra-s, and therefore make their own interpretation of the Veda-s, ignoring the śāstra. For example, one author states: "My contention is: only the Veda, that is given the status of apauruṣeya[27], has to state that it is not available or should be out of reach to the females, and not a historical pauruṣeya-text, i.e., any Dharmaśāstra, much less a Purāṇa."[28]

If this thought has come to the mind of any reader of this book, it might help to contemplate how the apauruṣeya Veda has reached us today in the classified form of four sacred texts. Do remember that the Veda-s in its current form has reached us through the work of Mahārṣi Vyāsa (Vedavyāsa), who is also the compiler of eighteen important purāṇa-s, the Mahābhārata, the Bhagvad Gītā, Śrīmad Bhāgavatam and even responsible for Parāśara smṛti (meant for kali yuga) based on the instructions of his father ṛṣi Parāśara. And this same Vedavyāsa states, at the beginning of Śrīmad Bhāgavatam, that it is being composed for the sake of those for whom the Veda-s are not meant, such as women, the śūdra varṇa and dvija-s who are so only by name.[29] Some of the most important purāṇa-s and śāstra-s have been composed by the same person who classified the Veda-s in this cycle of creation. How, then, can there be any difference in the thought process?

The śāstra-s and purāṇa-s are derived from the Veda-s and written in order to help us understand the Veda-s better and apply it

---

27 Apauruṣeya means that which has not come from man, meaning that it has a divine origin

28 Swamini Atmaprajnananda Saraswati in 'Ṛṣikās of the ṚgVeda.' Published in 2013.

29 Śrīmad Bhāgavatam (I.4.25) says that as the three Veda-s cannot be learnt by women, śūdras and dvija-s (who are so only by birth), the sage Vyāsa composed the story of Bhārata out of compassion for them. स्त्रीशूद्रद्विजबन्धूनां त्रयी न श्रुतिगोचरा । कर्मश्रेयसि मूढानां श्रेय एवं भवेदिह । इति भारतमाख्यानं कृपया मुनिना कृतम् ॥ २५ ॥

in the right way. The dharmaśāstra-s are the texts that lay down the rules for using the Veda-s. Therefore, there cannot be any question of picking one and rejecting the other.

Dharmaśāstra rules

In the paragraphs that follow, we will take a look at the rules mentioned in different dharmaśāstra texts and purāṇa-s pertaining to varṇa dharma, keeping in mind the eligibility for religious practices, particularly for women and the śūdra varṇa. In subsequent chapters of this book, as we explore the scientific basis of varṇa dharma, the purpose of the rules given here will become apparent.

Definition of varṇa

We begin with the definitions of varṇa as per different texts.

> i. From Manu (I.XVII, 1.31), we have the following definition of the origin of varṇa, which is similar to that of the Puruṣa Sūkta of the ṚgVeda (X.90.12):

लोकानां तु विवृद्ध्यर्थं मुखबाहूरुपादतः ।

ब्राह्मणं क्षत्रियं वैश्यं शूद्रं च निरवर्तयत् ॥ ३१ ॥

> 'With a view to the development of the (three) regions, He brought into existence the brāhmaṇa, the kṣatriya, the vaiśya and the śūdra, from out of His mouth, arms, thighs and feet (respectively).'— (31)

> ii. From Yājñavalkya Smṛti (I.10), we have the following definition, which talks about who among the four varṇa-s are considered as dvija (twice-born), thereby being eligible for mantra-based ceremonies:

ब्रह्मक्षत्रियविट्शूद्रा वर्णास्त्वाध्यास्त्रयो द्विजाः ।

निषेकाध्याः शमशानान्तास्तेषां वै मन्त्रतः क्रियाः ॥ १०॥

'The varṇa-s are the brāhmaṇa-s, the kṣatriya-s, the vaiśya-s and the śūdra-s. Of these, only the first three are dvija (twice-born); the performance of the ceremonies beginning with the rite (saṃskāra) of impregnation (garbhādhāna) and ending in the cremation ground (funeral rites of antyeṣṭi), of these (of dvija-s) alone are prescribed with mantra-s.'

iii. From Vasiṣṭha Dharmasūtra (Chapter 3, verse 2 & 3), we have what is similar to the Puruṣa Sūkta, but in addition there is the most interesting definition of varṇa in terms of metres (chandas), as follows:

ब्राह्मणोऽस्य मुखमासीद् बाहू राजन्यः कृतः ऊरू तदस्य यद्वैश्यः पद्भ्यां शूद्रो अजायत इत्यपि निगमो भवति २

गायत्र्या ब्राह्मणमसृजत त्रिष्टुभा राजन्यं जगत्या वैश्यं न केनचिच्छन्दसा शूद्रमित्यसंस्कार्यो विज्ञायते ३

There is also the following passage of the Veda, 'The brāhmaṇa was his mouth, the kṣatriya formed his arms, the vaiśya his thighs; the śūdra was born from his feet.'[2]

It has been declared in (the following passage of) the Veda that (a śūdra) shall not receive the sacraments, 'He created the brāhmaṇa with the gāyatrī (metre), the kṣatriya with the tṛṣṭubh, the vaiśya with the jagatī, the śūdra without any metre.'[3]

The eligibility for upanayana saṃskāra can thus be derived from the above definitions, which clearly excludes the śūdra varṇa. But what about girls/women?

Upanayana rules for girls/women

An individual's eligibility for the Vedic karma kāṇḍa comprising the saṃhita (the mantra-s in the Veda-s) and the araṇyaka (the rituals, ceremonies and yajña-s) is only for those who are eligible for the upanayana saṃskāra. Therefore, this is the first rule that we must look into before we discuss whether or not girls/women are eligible for Vedic mantra chanting, agni kriyā, etc.

iv. Quoting from Strīdharmapaddhati:

तत्र पुरुषाणामामौंजीबन्धनात् शास्त्रेण नियमाः न विधीयन्ते मौंजीबंधनप्रभृत्येव नियमाः ॥

'नास्य कर्म नियच्छन्नति किंचिदामौंजिबंधनात्' । 'प्रागुपनयनात् कामचारवादभक्षाः' ।

'उपनीय गुरुः शिष्यं शिक्षयेच्छौचमादितः । आचारमग्निकार्यं च सन्ध्योपासनमेव च ॥

इत्यादिवचनात् ॥

'For males, no rules are prescribed in śāstra-s till the time of upanayana. Adherence to rules begin with upanayana.' Thus says the following statements:

'Till upanayana, he has no rules prescribed for karma-s.' 'Before upanayana, travel, food and speech can be done as per his likes.'

'Guru performs upanayanam for the śiṣya and teaches him śaucācāra, agnikriyā (fire rituals) and sandyopāsanam (sandhya vandanam).'

स्त्रीणान्तु

वैवाहिको विधिः स्त्रीणामौपनयनिकः स्मृतः । पतिसेवा गुरौ वासो गृहार्थाग्निपरिक्रिया ॥

इति मनुवचनेन उपनयनस्थानापन्नो विवाह इति विवाहात् पूर्वं कामचारवादभक्षणं, विवाहानन्तरमेव नियमानुष्ठानम् । अतो वक्ष्यमाणधर्माः विवाहप्रभृत्येव ताभिरनुष्ठेयाः ॥

For women,

'Marriage is upanayana, service to husband is service to Guru and household chores are agnikriyā. With this statement of Manu (II.XV.67), marriage takes the place of upanayana in a woman's life. Travel, food and speech are as per her likes before marriage and rules are to be followed after marriage.'

While the code of Manu is considered as most relevant among smrti-s, and also included in Parāśara smrti, which is considered as the text meant for kali yuga, there are some scholars who point out that upanayana used to be done for women too in the earlier days, and that women used to wear the yajñopavīta (sacred thread).

v. This is perhaps owing to the below two verses citing Hārita and Yama, as mentioned in Smṛti Candrika (स्त्रीसंस्काराः) and also quoted in Smṛti Mukta Phalam from the same source,[30] as follows:

यत्तु हारीतेनोक्तं -

'द्विविधास्त्रियो ब्रह्मवादिन्यः सधोवध्वश्च । तत्र ब्रह्मवादिनीनामुपन यनमग्नीन्धनं वेदाध्ययनं स्वगृहे च भिक्षाचर्येति । सध्योवधूनां चोपस्थिते विवाहे कथम्चिदुपनयनमात्रम् कृत्वा विवाहः कार्यः'

इति । तत्कल्पान्तराभिप्रायं । तथा च यमः-

पुरा कल्पे तु नारीणां मौन्जीबन्धनमिष्यते।

अध्यापनं च वेदानां सवित्रीवचनं तथा।।

पिता पितृव्यो भ्राता वा नैनामध्यापयेत्परः।

स्वगृहे चैव कन्यायाः भैक्षचर्या विधीयते ।।

वर्जयेदजिनं चीरं जटाधारणमेव च।।

The interpretation of the above verses in Smṛti Mukta Phalam[31] is given as follows:

'Women are of two types, Brahmavādini & Sadyovadu. Of them, for Brahmavādini-s, upanayanam, agni kāryam,

---

30 Since there is no text of Hārita on Dharmasūtra available in either print or manuscript form, one has to rely on this text quoted by others.

31 Smriti Mukta Phalam, Varnashrama Dharma Kanda, Sri Vaidyanatha Dikshitar, translated by P.R. Kannan

study of Veda-s and living on alms in their own home are prescribed. For sadyovadu, 'upanayanam should be done at the time of marriage, prior to marriage ceremony,' this refers to the previous kalpa.

In a similar vein, Yama says that 'in the previous kalpa, for women also, upanayanam, the study of Veda-s and Gāyatrī japa were prescribed. None other than father, his brother and her own brother should teach Veda to women. They should live on alms in their own homes. Deerskin, the bark of a tree and matted hair should not be worn by women.'

Do note that in both the above verses, it is mentioned that this practice existed in another kalpa.[32] Although these references can easily be ignored as it is not mentioned in the smṛti meant for our kalpa, we will touch upon this in further detail in the section on exceptions after having explored the subtle principles and science behind the primary rules.

Saṃskāra rules for women

While the absence of upanayana for women and the śūdra varṇa is fairly clear, we find that most of the other saṃskāra-s are performed for women and the śūdra varṇa as well, but without mantra-s. The exception is that for women (who are not of the śūdra varṇa),

---

32 A kalpa is a day of Brahmā, and one day of Brahmā consists of 14 Manvantara-s.

Explanation: The age of Kali is said to be 4,32,000 years. Twice this is the age of Dvāpara. Three times Kali is the age of Tretā. Four times Kali is the age of Satya yuga. Together they make a chaturyuga (43,20,000 years). If 71 such cycles go by, it is considered as one Manvantara, which is the lifespan of one Manu. If 14 Manvantara-s pass by, it is one day of Brahma, which is called a kalpa. Source: Youtube talk by Swami Mukundananda titled 'What Vedas say about time will change your view of the universe', featured in the official channel of Swami Mukundananda.

mantra-s are allowed during the vivāha saṃskāra (marriage). This is mentioned in the below verses:

vi. Manu, Yājñavalkya, Gobhila and other texts mention that karma-s from Jātakarma till Chaula should be done for female children without mantra and marriage with mantra. This is cited in the below verses:

Manu states (II.XV.66),

अमन्त्रिका तु कार्य्येयं स्त्रीणामावृदशेषतः ।

संस्काराथं शरीरस्य यथाकालं यथाक्रमम् ॥ ६६ ॥

'For females, this whole series (the saṃskāra-s) should be performed at the right time and in the proper order, for the purpose of sanctifying the body; but without the Vedic formulas.'— (66)

Yājñavalkya, 1.13.— 'These rites for women are to be performed silently, but marriage is to be with mantra-s.'

Viṣṇu-Smṛti, 27.13.— 'The same rites for women are done without mantra-s.'

Āśvalāyana-Gṛhyasūtra, 15 (16.7)—1.2. — 'For the girl, the āvṛta only' ('āvṛta' standing for the Jātakarma and other rites)

Gobhila-Gṛhyasūtra (Vīramitrodaya-Saṃskāra, p. 191). — 'For women, these rites are to be performed silently, but the homa is to be done with mantra-s.'

Śaunaka (Do., p. 278). — 'All this rite is to be performed for the girl, without mantra.'

Saṃskāra rules for śūdra varṇa

Let us also take a look at the verses which mention the rules for the śūdra varṇa with respect to other saṃskāra-s.

vii. Manu (X.10.127) has mentioned that while śūdra-s can imitate the behaviour of others (dvija-s), they should not recite the sacred texts, i.e. all religious rites are for the śūdra without Vedic chanting:

धर्मेप्सवस्तु धर्मज्ञाः सतां वृत्तमनुष्ठिताः ।

मन्त्रवर्ज्यं न दुष्यन्ति प्रशंसां प्राप्नुवन्ति च ॥ १२७ ॥

'If those who, knowing their duty, and wishing to acquire merit, imitate the practices of righteous men, with the exception of reciting the sacred texts, they incur no guilt; they obtain praise.' — (127)

viii. Similarly, we find Sankha (as quoted by Vishwarupa on Yaj. I. 13) opines that saṃskāra-s may be performed for śūdra-s but without Vedic mantra-s.

ix. Vedavyāsa (I.17) prescribes that the saṃskāra-s (viz., garbhādhāna, puṃsavana, sīmantonnayana, jātakarma, nāmakaraṇa, niṣkramaṇa, annaprāśana, caula, karṇavedha and vivāha) can be performed in the case of śūdra, but without Vedic mantra. Haradatta on Gautama X.51 says the same.

When we observe the rules for the saṃskāra-s for women and the śūdra varṇa, we see that it is very similar, with the exception that vivāha is done with mantra-s for women (who are not of the śūdra varṇa), and this vivāha is considered as equivalent to the upanayana. Therefore, it is also interesting that after marriage, a woman becomes eligible to perform some of the agnikriyā-s with her husband. In fact, it is stated as the right of a married woman to perform these. So, let us take a look at the rules for a woman after marriage.

Aupāsana & Agnihotra rules for married women

Let us now look at the dharmaśāstra rules pertaining to agnihotra and aupāsana for women after marriage:

x. Manu (V.XIV, 5.151) says that it is through her husband that a woman is entitled to perform religious acts and obtain the happiness gained through that.

अनृतावृतुकाले च मन्त्रसंस्कारकृत् पतिः ।

सुखस्य नित्यं दातैह परलोके च योषितः ॥ १५१ ॥

'The husband who has performed the mantric sacramental rites for women is the imparter of happiness to them both in season and out of season, here as well as in the next world.' — (151).

xi. Manu (V.XIV. 5.153) and Viṣṇu Dharmasūtra (25.15) state the same rules that there are no separate religious acts for women apart from what she is entitled to perform with her husband.

नास्ति स्त्रीणां पृथग् यज्ञो न व्रतं नाप्युपोषणम् ।

पतिं शुश्रूषते येन तेन स्वर्गे महीयते ॥ १५३ ॥

'There is no separate yajña (sacrificing) for women, nor vrata (vows), nor fasts (without his consent); it is by means of serving her husband that she becomes exalted in heaven.' — (153).

xii. Manu (III.3.121) says that from the food cooked in the evening, the wife should offer bali-s, but without mantra-s.

सायं त्वन्नस्य सिद्धस्य पत्न्यमन्त्रं बलिं हरेत् ।

वैश्वदेवं हि नामैतत् सायं प्रातर्विधीयते ॥ १२१ ॥

'Out of the food cooked in the evening the wife should offer the bali (oblation), without sacred formulas (meaning, without mantra). This is the Vaiśvadeva rite which has been enjoined for both morning and evening.'— (121)

The commentator Medhātithi points out that when it is said, 'without sacred formulas' what is interdicted is the use of expressions containing the names of the deity and ending with the syllable 'svāhā'; such expressions, for instance, as 'agnaye svāhā', and the like; no other sacred formulas have been prescribed in connection with the Vaiśvadeva offerings. He further says that verbal reference to the gods being prohibited, the wife shall make the reference mentally.

Note that other commentators, such as Ganganath Jha, have specifically stated that 'Vaiśvadeva' here refers only to the bali and not to the performance of homa, which is forbidden for women. The verse is also quoted in Vīramitrodaya (Āhnika, p. 403), which adds the following explanation: Bali offering without mantra-s, with food cooked in the evening, is to be done by the wife only in the absence of the householder and his sons; 'homa' by women being generally interdicted by several texts.

xiii. The Trikāṇḍamaṇḍana (I.80-81 and 85)[33] says that when the husband is gone abroad, the wife may, with the help of a priest, perform the daily duties of agnihotra, the obligatory iṣṭi and pitṛyajña, but should not perform soma sacrifices.

अतोग्निहोत्रं नित्येष्टिः पितृयज्ञ इति त्रयम् ।

कर्तव्यं प्रोषिते पत्यौ नान्यत्स्वामि - क्रियान्वितम् ।

त्रिकाण्डमण्डन I. 83.

Finally, let us summarise the agnihotra rules for women by sharing verses from Strīdharmapaddhati:

xiv. Āśvalāyana (for followers of Ṛgveda) states thus:

तथा चाश्वलायनः -

'पाणिग्रहणादि गृह्यं परिचरेत् स्वयं पत्न्यपि वा पुत्रः कुमार्यन्तेवासी वा' इति ॥

---

33 Vide Part I, Vol II of 'History of Dharmaśāstra' by Dr. P.V. Kane, Chapter X1, Page 566

'After Pānigrahana (an important segment in Vedic marriage), one should do agni śuśruṣā (upkeep the agni). One's wife, son, daughter or disciple can also take care of this agni.'

xv. Āpastamba (for followers of Krishna Yajur Veda) states:

पत्न्यास्तु - 'पत्नीवदस्याग्निहोत्रं भवती' त्यापस्तम्बाचार्यैः अग्निहोत्रे पत्नीसंबन्धनियमनात् अग्निहोत्रं विहाय कुत्रापि न स्थेयम् । अग्निहोत्र एव सर्वतीर्थफलावगमाच ॥

'Agnihotra is only for the one who has a wife.' As Agnihotra is related to one's wife (is done along with), he should not stay away from his home leaving the agni. Agnihotra itself will bring the fruits of all tīrtha (holy places).

xvi. Bodhāyana (for followers of Kṛṣṇa Yajur Veda) states:

बोधायनस्तु उद्धरणानन्तरमेवोपवेशनमाह -- सायंप्रातरेवैषा पत्न्यन्वास्ते इति ॥

होमे तूभयोः सन्निधानं मुख्यम् । यजमानासन्निधाने पत्न्या अवश्यं सन्निहितया भवितव्यम् ।

'One should sit only after lighting agni. Patni (wife) will accompany in the morning and evening. In homa, both husband and wife should be present. If Yajamāna (man who performs the ritual) is not present, it is imperative for his wife to be present.'

xvii. Katyāyana states:

तथा च कात्यायनः

असमक्षं तु दम्पत्योर्होतव्यं नर्त्विगादिना ।

द्वयोरप्यसमक्षं तु भवेद्धुतमनर्थकम् ॥

निक्षिप्याग्निं स्वदारेषु परिकल्प्यविजं तथा ।

प्रवसेत् कार्यवान्विप्रो न वृथैव चिरं वसेत् ॥ ८३ ॥

'Ṛtvik-s (priests) should not perform the sacrifice without the presence of the couple (dampati). If both are absent then the homa is worthless. One can go out of station after handing over the agni to his wife and arrange the ṛtvik to perform the ritual. Stationing abroad should be done with a purpose and one should not stay more than that is required for the purpose.'

Rules related to the wife are similar for aupāsana also.

xviii.   अयं च पत्नीसंबन्धनियमः औपासनेऽपि तुल्यः ॥

'Homa-s performed in the absence of both (husband and wife) is fruitless.'

'द्वयोरप्यसमक्षं तु भवेद्धुतमनर्थक' मिति पूर्वक्तकात्यायन वचनस्य साधारणत्वात् ॥

'This statement of Katyāyana is common to aupāsana and agnihotra.'

xix.   अग्निहोत्रहोमे 'तस्मादग्हिोत्रस्य यज्ञक्रतो रेक ऋत्विक', 'स्वयं पर्वणि जुहुयात् ऋत्विजमेक इतरं काल' मिति श्रुतिसूत्राभ्यां ऋत्विग्यजमानयोरेव नियमनात् पत्न्याः कर्तृत्वप्रसक्तिरेव नास्ति ।

In agnihotra homa, 'for agnihotra there is only one ṛtvik. Do it by oneself during parvas and have one ṛtvik otherwise.' Since the śruti-s have made things clear on the role of yajamāna and ṛtvik, the question of ownership of the wife (alone) doesn't arise.

xx.   Āpastamba prohibits homa for women, while stating about aupāsana,

औपसनहोमेऽपि 'स्त्रियाऽनुपेतेन क्षारलवणावरान्नसंसृष्टस्य च होमं परिचक्षते' इत्यापस्तम्बाचार्यैः कर्तृत्वं प्रतिषिद्धम् ।

'Women and boys who haven't undergone upanayana shouldn't perform homa. Dravya-s that are sour, salty, and poor-quality rice shouldn't be used.'

Other religious activities for women and the śūdra varṇa

Pilgrimage: With the current trend of people of all ages visiting mokṣa dhām-s, it is important to understand that visits to tīrtha kṣhetram were not included as part of the rules for householders. In fact, the śāstra-s explicitly prohibit such visits for the householder, both men and women, as seen in the following verses.

xxi. 'यस्येष्टिधर्मेष्वधिकारिताऽस्ति वरं गृहं गृहधर्माश्च सर्वे ।

एवं गृहस्थाश्रमसंस्थितस्य तिर्थं गतिः पूर्वतरैर्निषिद्ध।' इति वचनेन तीर्थार्थं प्रवासः प्रतिषिद्धयते ॥ ८४

'One who has adhikāra (right) to perform iṣṭi (sacrifices), for him, his home and his duties are of prime importance. Ancestors have not allowed pilgrimage for householders.' This means that pravāsa (travel) is not allowed for the sake of pilgrimage (for householders).

xxii. The Tīrtha Prabandha says:

जपस्तपस्तीर्थयात्रा प्रव्रज्या मन्त्रसाधनम् । देवताराधनं चेति स्त्रीशूद्रपतनानि षट्॥ q. by तीर्थप्र. P.21

'Japa, tapas, pilgrimage to holy places (tīrtha yātra), becoming an ascetic (sanyasin), efforts to attain mastery over mantra-s and worshipping of deities (as a priest) – these six lead to sinfulness in the case of women and śūdra-s.'

xxiii. Similarly, Atri (136-137) says:

अतः परं प्रवक्ष्यामि स्त्रीशूद्रपतनानि च । जपस्तपस्तीर्थयात्रा प्रव्रज्या मन्त्र- साधनम् । देवताराधनं चैव स्त्रीशूद्रपतनानि षट् । अत्रि 136-137.

'Six actions by women and śūdra-s lead to sinfulness, viz., japa, tapas (austerities), pravrajyā (ascetic's life), pilgrimages, endeavour to secure miraculous power by repeating spells, sole devotion to the worship of a deity.'[34]

---

34 Vide 'History of Dharmaśāstra' by Dr. P.V. Kane, Volume II, Part II, Ch. XXVIII, Page 945

This means that such activities might not bear any positive results for women and the śūdra varṇa, and 'leading to sinfulness' means that it will result in a negative impact. This is very much what we will understand when we decode the biological basis for this rule in the subsequent chapters of this book.

Eligibility for mantra chanting

From Śūdrakamalākara, we have the following guidelines regarding chanting of mantra-s for śūdra-s and women:

xxiv. अथ शूद्रस्य मन्त्रविचारः ॥ तत्र अविद्यत्वाद्वेदमन्त्रे नाधिकारः ॥ व्यासोपि ॥ शूद्रो वर्णश्चतुर्थोऽपि वर्णत्वाद्धर्ममर्हति ॥ वेदमंत्रस्वधास्वाहा वषट्कारादिभिर्विनेति ॥ [व्या० स्मृ० अ० १ ० ६]

'Regarding mantra eligibility for śūdra-s, because there is no Vedic education (no upanayanam) for śūdra-s, they have no eligibility for mantra-s. Even though Vyāsa has said that śūdra-s are also part of the four varṇa-s and varṇa dharma applies to them as well, that are not entitled to self-study of Veda, mantra japa, pitṛ karma, homa, śrauta karma/yāga, etc.'

xxv. नृसिंहतापिनीये ॥ सावित्रीं प्रणवं यजुर्लक्ष्मीं स्त्रीशूद्राय नेच्छति ॥ पराशरभाप्येप्येवम् ॥ रामतापिनीये ॥ सावित्रीं लक्ष्मीं यजुः प्रणवं यदि जानीयात्स्त्रीशूद्रः स मृतोधो गच्छति ॥

'As per Nṛsiṃha Tāpanīya Upaniṣad, the Savitri mantra (as given in Yajur Veda), praṇava (om), Yajur Lakṣmī[35] — these are not desirable for women and śūdra-s. Parāśara has also said this. In Rāma Tāpanīya Upaniṣad, it is said that if women or śūdra-s learn Savitri, lakshmim (Śrī bījam), yajuh praṇava, after death, they will go to adholoka (lower worlds/ realms).'

---

35 Yajur Mahālakṣmī Mantra as given in the Nṛsiṃha Tapanīya Upaniṣad is 'om bhūr lakṣmī, bhuvar lakṣmī, suva kala karni, thanno lakṣmī pracodayat'

xxvi. गौडनिबन्धे तिथितत्त्वे स्कान्दे ॥ स्वाहा प्रणव संयुक्तं शुभे मनं ददद्विजः ॥ शूद्रो निरयमामोति ब्रह्मणः शुद्धतामियात् ॥ एवं पुराणविष्णु- सहस्नामचण्डीस्तोत्रादिपाठेप्यनधिकारः ॥

'In Gauḍanibandha, Tithitattva and Skanda Purāṇa, it is said that if svāhā mantra-s or praṇava mantra-s are given by a brāhmaṇa to a śūdra, then the śūdra will go to naraka and the brāhmaṇa will become a śūdra. Thus, there is no adhikāra for purāṇa, Viṣṇu Sahasranāma, chandi stotram chanting, etc. for women and śūdra-s.'

xxvii. श्रवणमात्रेऽधिकारेण पाठाप्रसक्तेः ॥ तदुक्तं हरिवंशे ॥

'They have adhikāra only for śravaṇa (listening), not for chanting. This is told in Harivamsha.'

xxviii. सुगतिमियाच्छ्रवणाच्च शूद्रजातिरिति ॥ अतएव भारते विष्णुसहस्नामसु ॥ वेदान्तगो ब्राह्मणः स्यात्क्षत्रियो विजयी भवेत् ॥ वैश्यो धनसमृद्धः स्याच्छूद्रः सुखमवामुयात् ॥ [म० भा० अ० प० वि० श्लो० १-३] इत्यत्र शुद्रः श्रवणेनैवेति शङ्करराचार्यैव्याख्यातम् ॥

'(With śravaṇa alone) śūdra will attain happiness and this is what is meant in the phala śruti portion of Viṣṇu Sahasranāma which says that by listening to the sahasranāma, brāhmaṇa-s will attain knowledge of the Veda, kṣatriya-s will attain victory, vaiśya-s will obtain wealth, and śūdra-s will obtain happiness. This is (also) mentioned in Śrī Śankarācārya's bhāṣyaṃ', as follows,

तत्रैव हरिवंशवचनमाह सुगतिमिति । तथा च स्त्रीशूद्राणामितिहासपुराण गतस्तवपठने नाविकार इति भावः ॥ १२३ ॥, meaning 'women and śūdra-s have no adhikāra to chant anything which is a part of Ithihāsa, purāṇa-s. Hence, Viṣṇu Sahasranāma, chandi etc. are prohibited to be chanted by śūdra-s and women.'

xxix. अमन्त्रस्येति विशेषणात् स्त्रीणां तत्तुल्यानां चेति शूलपाणिः

Shoolapani says all these are applicable to women.

While the dharmaśāstra rules are clear about the prohibition of Vedic mantra chanting for women and the śūdra varṇa, there is some modification that can be made by simplifying the chants, as given in the below verses of the Śūdrakamalākara:

xxx.   'All persons, including the śūdra-s and even caṇḍāla-s were authorised to repeat the Rāmamantra of 13 letters (Śrī Rām jaya Rām jaya jaya Rām), and the Śiva mantra of 5 letters (namaḥ śivāya), while dvijati-s could repeat the Śiva mantra of six letters (om namaḥ śivāya).'[36]

Other religious rights of the śūdra varṇa

The śūdra varṇa was allowed to perform the five daily sacrifices called Mahāyajña-s in the ordinary fire. He could perform śraddhā. He was to think of the devatā-s and utter loudly the word 'namaḥ', which was to be the only mantra in his case (i.e. he was not to say 'agnaye svāhā) but to think of agni and say 'namaḥ.' This is conveyed in the following verses:[37]

xxxi.   अनुज्ञातोऽस्य नमस्कारो मन्त्रः । पाकयज्ञैः स्वयं यजेतेत्येके । गौ. 10. 66-67;

xxxii.   पञ्चयज्ञविधानं तु शूद्रस्यापि विधीयते । तस्य प्रोक्तो नमस्कारः कुर्वन्नित्यं न हीयते ॥ लघुविष्णु V. 9

xxxiii.   दानं च दद्याच्छूद्रोपि पाकयज्ञैर्यजेत च । पित्र्यादिकं च वै सर्वे शूद्रः कुर्वीत तेन वै ॥ विष्णुपुराण III. 8. 33;

xxxiv.   स्वाहाकारवषट्कारौ मन्त्रः शूद्रे न विद्यते । तस्माच्छूद्रः पाकयज्ञैर्यजेताव्रतवान् स्ययम् ॥ शान्तिपर्व 60. 37-38;

Study of religious texts: While the study of the Veda-s was not for the śūdra varṇa and women, since they were not eligible for upanayana,

---

36 This is taken from the English translation of the corresponding verses of the Sudrakamalākara, by Dr. Kane in 'History of Dharmaśāstra' Part 1, Vol II, Ch. III, Page 158

37 Vide 'History of Dharmaśāstra' Part 1, Vol II, Ch. III, Page 158

they were encouraged to study the purāṇa-s, itihāsa and smṛti texts, by listening to it from a brāhmaṇa.

xxxv. Śrīmad Bhāgavatam (I.4.25) says that as the three Veda-s cannot be chanted by women, śūdra-s and dvija-s (who are so only by birth), the sage Vyāsa composed the story of Bhārata out of compassion for them.

स्त्रीशूद्रद्विजबन्धूनां त्रयी न श्रुतिगोचरा ।

कर्मश्रेयसि मूढानां श्रेय एवं भवेदिह ।

इति भारतमाख्यानं कृपया मुनिना कृतम् ॥ २५ ॥

xxxvi. Śankarācārya on Vedānta Sūtra (I.3.38) quotes Śānti 328.49 and says that the śūdra has no adhikāra (eligibility) for brahmavidyā based upon a study of the Veda, but that a śūdra can attain spiritual development (just as Vidura & Dharmavyādha mentioned in Mahābhāratha did) and that he may attain to mokṣa, the fruit of correct knowledge, through the hearing of purāṇa-s and study of other texts like the Bhagvad Gītā, etc.

Officiating in temples

With the rights-based movement picking up pace, demanding that women and the śūdra varṇa be allowed to perform temple rituals, it is important to understand the rules stated on this matter.

Regarding the prāṇa pratiṣṭhā (ritual consecration) done for a temple, the following texts have mentioned a few rules in this regard:

xxxvii. The Tristhalīsetu (of Nārāyaṇa) quotes a passage of the Bṛhan-Nāradīya Purāṇa to the effect that women, those whose upanayana has not been performed, and śūdra-s have no eligibility to establish the images of Viṣṇu or Śiva.[38]

---

38 Vide History of Dharmaśāstra' by Dr. Kane, Part 1 Vol II, Chapter XII, Page 595

xxxviii. The Devapratiṣṭhātattva (p.505) quotes the Hayaśirṣa Pañcarātra to the effect that generally a brāhmaṇa should officiate at the consecration (prāṇa pratiṣṭhā) of an image of Viṣṇu, but a kṣatriya can officiate for a vaiśya or a śūdra yajamāna, and a vaiśya may do for a śūdra yajamāna, but a śūdra cannot officiate.[39]

The importance of this rule is emphasised by the fact that if, in case, a pratiṣṭhāpita mūrti has been touched by those who should not do so, the prāṇa pratiṣṭhā process has to be done once again, as mentioned below.

xxxix. 'If an image properly consecrated has had no worship performed without pre-meditation (i.e. owing to forgetfulness or neglect) for one night or a month or two months or the image is touched by a śūdra or a woman in her monthly menses, then the image should have water adhivasa (placing in water) performed on it, and it should be bathed with water from a jar, then with pañcagavya, then it should be bathed with pure water from jars to the accompaniment of the hymn to Puruṣa (Ṛg. X. 90) repeated 8000 times, 800 times or 28 times, worship should be offered with sandal-wood paste and flowers, naivedyam (food) of rice cooked with jaggery should be offered. This is the way in which the re-consecration is effected.'[40]

Regarding who can offer pūjā, we have the following rules:

xl. Regarding Devayajña (pūjā offered to an image), Vṛddha-Hārīta (VIII. 183-189) highly extols Salagrama-pūjā. It is stated by Vṛddha-Hārīta that only dvija-s can worship Salagrāma and not śūdra-s.

---

39 Vide History of Dharmaśāstra' by Dr. Kane, Part II, Vol II, Ch. XXVI, Page 900

40 Vide History of Dharmaśāstra' by Dr. Kane, Part II, Vol II, Ch. XXVI, Page 905

द्विजानामेव नान्येषां शालग्रामशिलार्चनम् । वृद्धहारीत VIII. 190.[41]

xli. According to some passages quoted in the Pūjāprakāśa (pp. 20-21) even women and śūdra-s can perform the worship of Salagràma, but they should not touch it. Similarly, they are not to worship linga-s established in the past by sages, etc.

शालग्रामशिला यत्र यत्र द्वारवतीशिला । उभयो: संगमो यत्र तत्र मुक्तिर्न संशयः ॥ नारद quoted in स्मृतिमु. (आह्निक p. 384); vide also पूजा-प्रकाश. p. 11 and आचाररत्न p. 78a quoting स्कन्दपुराण.

xlii. In the case of the fierce form of Nārasiṃha, the texts mention that all are eligible to offer pūjā, as given below.

ब्राह्मणाः क्षत्रिया वैश्याः स्त्रियः शूद्रान्त्यजातयः । संपूज्य तं सुरश्रेष्ठं भक्त्या सिंहवपुर्धरम् । मुच्यन्ते चाशुभैर्दु:खैर्जन्मकोटि समुद्भवैः । नृसिंहपुराण quoted in पूजा-प्रकाश p. 1, शूद्रकमलाकर p. 33

'Brāhmaṇa, kṣatriya, vaiśya, women, śūdra and even the antyaja (those jāti-s below a śūdra) were to worship Viṣṇu who incarnated himself as man-lion, according to the Nrsimhapurāṇa and Vṛddha-Hārīta (VI. 6 and 256).'

xliii. In Śrīmad Bhāgavatam (11.27.7), Bhagavān Śrī Kṛṣṇa himself explains the ways in which he can receive offerings:

वैदिकस्तान्त्रिको मिश्र इति मे त्रिविधो मख: ।

त्रयाणामीप्सितेनैव विधिना मां समर्चरेत् ॥ ७ ॥

'One should carefully worship Me by selecting one of the three methods by which I receive sacrifice: vaidikah, tāntrikah or miśrah (mixed).'

Some of the commentators[42] state that 'vaidikah' refers to sacrifice performed with mantra-s from the four Veda-s and

---

41 Vide History of Dharmaśāstra' by Dr. Kane, Part II, Vol II, Ch. XIX, Page 716

42 The Agama Encyclopaedia by S.K. Ramachandra Rao, and the commentary on Śrīmad Bhāgavatam in www.Vedabase.io both provide the above explanation for the verse.

auxiliary Vedic literature. 'Tāntrika' refers to such literature as the Pañcarātra. And 'miśraḥ' or mixed indicates utilisation of both kinds of literature. In the very next verse in Śrīmad Bhāgavatam (11.27.8), Bhagavān explains the step-by-step method by which this is to be done, stating that it is for the dvija-s (meaning, it is not for others), as given below:

यदा स्वनिगमेनोक्तं द्विजत्वं प्राप्य पूरुष: ।

यथा यजेत मां भक्त्या श्रद्धया तन्निबोध मे ॥ ८ ॥

'Now please listen faithfully as I explain exactly how a person who has achieved twice-born status through the relevant Vedic prescriptions should worship Me with devotion.'

Śabda Pramāṇa

When there is doubt about certain rules, the śabda pramāṇa offered by dharma śāstra texts and also what is mentioned in the purāṇa-s are to be considered as having the final authority. However, there is a tendency among many who have modified the rules in their lives or intend to do so to dismiss what is given in the dharmaśāstra-s by saying that these are ancient rules which are no longer relevant for our times. If that is the case, then surely, this system would have been called Purātana Dharma (ancient dharma). But instead, every Hindu takes pride in calling it Sanātana Dharma, meaning that dharma which is sanātana or sadā nūtana (always new), meaning it is eternal and applicable for all times.

For those who might still feel that these texts are ancient and need not be followed in modern times, let us at least take seriously the words of learned men of recent times, summarising the rules for women:

"Women, who have been born in brāhmaṇa, kṣatriya or vaiśya varṇa and have been married as per tradition, they do not need a separate yajñopavīta saṃskāra. They are authorised to listen to Veda-s and mantra-s inside the yajñashala by sitting to the right side of the husband who would have already got his yajñopavita done. The women (wife) do not offer āhūti, but whatever karma is done by the husband, is successful/ accomplished only due to the presence of the wife. That is why, the presence of the wife is crucial for performance of these."

– Recorded from a talk by the current
Śaṅkarācārya of Govardhan Puri Peeth, His Holiness
Swami Śrī Nischalānanda Saraswati-ji

"Those who complain that women have no right to perform yajña on their own must remember that men too have no right to the same without a wife. This is according to the Veda-s themself (patni-vathasya agnihotram bhavati). Marriage or vivāha is known as saha-dharma-charini-samprayōgam. It means the noble union of a man with a lady who will practice dharma along with him - that is why she is called dharma-patni......Only a householder with a wife may perform yajña-s, not student-bachelors and ascetics."

– His Holiness Śrī Chandraśekharendra Saraswati
(Kanchi Kamakoti Pītham), also known as
Mahāperiyavā - talk on 'The High Status of Our Women',
recorded in the book 'Voice of God'

In summarising what is allowed and disallowed for women, there are also the following words of Śrī Rajarshi Nandi, a recognised scholar and practitioner of tantra, sent via email on July 3rd, 2021, when requested to summarise the traditional rules for mantra chanting for women:

"To find mantra-s which are traditionally disallowed for women is actually quite easy. All kinds of Vedic karma kāṇda is not allowed for women, only men who are gṛhasta-s, that is married, are allowed to perform the karma kāṇda part. Jñāna kāṇda (upanishadic knowledge, etc.) is allowed for all men and women, (whereas) karma kāṇda has restrictions. Even all men cannot perform karma kāṇda. So fire rituals in the Vedic system are all disallowed for women. This is quite in contravention to modern day organisations which promote fire rituals for everyone. In fact recitation of Vedic mantra-s are also not encouraged for women, that is, mantra-s from the core Veda saṃhita. That includes common things like Gāyatrī mantra, Mahāmṛtyuñjaya (the Vedic version of it), etc.

In all, organisations that promote indiscriminate fire rituals for all, are also not in tune with the traditional ideas. Only fire rituals that women were asked to participate in was the aupāsana agni after marriage, but it is a very limited ritual engagement with fire, unlike homa, etc.

In the tantric system, as noted, these restrictions are not there, but there is an entry bar in terms of dīkṣā and adhikāra. All men and women are allowed to do most rituals and in fact, in deeper sādhanā, in some aspects women get precedence in some types of sādhanā, but those are not in common domain. Even in tantric system some texts mention that women need not do fire rituals at all and only japa is enough to give the fruits of the sādhanā.

So, in short, all Vedic mantras (those that come from the Vedic saṃhita, not Upanishadic literature) are by and large not allowed for women to chant unless it is allowed in an individual's case by a guru or (by virtue of a) siddhi, but that is not the norm. Fire rituals are even more disallowed. (Even in the tantric systems, there are restrictions for both men and women)."

Let us end this chapter with important words of wisdom from Bhagavān Śrī Kṛṣṇa, as recorded in the Bhagvad Gītā (16.23):

य: शास्त्रविधिमुत्सृज्य वर्तते कामकारत: |

न स सिद्धिमवाप्नोति न सुखं न परां गतिम् || 23||

'Those who act under the impulse of desire, discarding the injunctions of the scriptures, attain neither perfection, nor happiness, nor the supreme goal in life.'

Self-Examination

Swami Chinmayānanda said that there are three kinds of vāsana-s: Loka vāsana, Deha vāsana and Śāstra vāsana. This important quote by Swamiji is a timely reminder for us to introspect and to be aware of what not to carry into this book as we journey to explore the deep science behind the injunctions of the śāstra-s.

'Loka Vāsana is the clinging attachment to the world of name, fame, wealth, identification with the community, society and all other.' If we have this vāsana, our mind will manipulate all that we read to make it suitable to upkeep the image we have presented to the world. When unlearning becomes difficult, re-learning does not happen.

'Deha Vāsana is when one is busy pampering the body and having no time to contemplate.' This could also happen if one is unwell or in physical pain and, therefore, unable to go beyond body awareness. If this vāsana dominates, then we might not even have the ability to sit still and read, let alone contemplate. If our awareness is firmly rooted in the body and its identity, higher learning cannot happen.

'Śāstra Vāsana happens when we study the śāstra-s without understanding the depth and implied subtle suggestions and by only understanding the superficial meaning.' Emerging from the previous chapter, which quoted several rules from the śāstra-s, this is something that we need to become mindful of. Even if we read just one verse from any śāstra, let us strive to understand it in all its subtility.

The verses from the śāstra-s shared in the previous chapter are negligible in number compared to the vast volumes of texts of dharmaśāstra, but by knowing even these few verses in their subtility, we will see that light will dawn on several of the injunctions in the śāstra-s. Without knowing these, no matter how many śāstra-s one reads and quotes, all we will acquire is śāstra-vāsana.

Chapter 3: Varṇa as Colour

In the introduction of this book, there was a mention of Devī's names with the word varṇa, and that this could mean varṇa as colour or varṇa as sound. Let us first explore varṇa as colour, and in the next chapter, we will look at varṇa as sound.

Light

What the human eye perceives as colour is nothing but an electromagnetic wave occurring in the visible spectrum of the larger electromagnetic spectrum. Instead of referring to colours technically as electromagnetic radiation having specific wavelengths and frequencies, we can also just refer to it as light. So, varṇa, which means colour, is also light.

Interestingly, the earliest mention of the word varṇa in the ṚgVeda, uses this word to mean light (I.73.7, II.3.5, IX.97.15, IX.104.4).[43] We further see that varṇa is also used to indicate the devatā-s such as Varuṇā (ṚgVeda X.124.7) as having a pure or bright (śucayo) varṇa, while the asura-a and rākṣasa-s are described as being of dark (kṛṣṇa) varṇa or asura varṇa (ṚgVeda IX. 71.2, I. 130.8, IV.16.13, IX.41.1). Some commentators assume that the word varṇa in these verses indicate the colour of the skin of devatā-s and asura-s. Given that we have Bhagavān Śrī Kṛṣṇa, a dark-skinned Lord having the name Kṛṣṇa also because of his dark skin, and yet not being an asura, it is fairly safe to say that the ṚgVeda texts were also not

---

43 Vide 'History of Dharmaśāstra' Vol II, Part 1, by Dr. P.V. Kane.

referring to kṛṣṇa varṇa as the skin colour of the asura-s. What, then, did they mean by varṇa?

Aura

If we understand varṇa as light as indicated in some verses of the ṚgVeda, we will arrive at a different meaning here — varṇa is used to indicate the beings of bright light (śucayo varṇam) and the beings without light (kṛṣṇa varṇam). In other words, they are referring to the aura of devatā-s like Varunā, which showed pure/bright light, and the aura of beings called asura or rākṣasa, who had the absence of light and hence appeared dark. This also falls in line with the technical understanding of the colour black (kṛṣṇa varṇa) or of darkness, which is not a colour on its own but rather the absence of light. Thus, we have varṇa as colour or light, not of the skin, but of the aura. This is a reference to the subtle aura that the enlightened ṛṣi-s were able to see. This is also evidenced in the traditional artwork of all religions — the devatā-s are shown with a bright halo around their head, while the rākṣasa-s or demons do not have such a halo.

The ṛṣi-s who codified the Veda and śāstra were enlightened beings. Through their siddhi (spiritual ability), they easily perceived the subtle realm. When they looked at humans, or for that matter, at all of life, they saw the aura as easily as we see the physical form. Therefore, what they wrote was from this vision of the subtle aura that they saw and experienced.

Being able to see the aura of people or things is not very difficult. With a little guidance, most people who can sit still for a few minutes and focus can learn to see the aura. In such cases, it would be seen as a light surrounding a person or thing. We will be able to see that this light is minimal and dim in a person who is worldly-minded, and we will also be able to see that this light extends a few inches above one's head and/or sideways in people who are sattvic or practice some form of sādhanā. In Guru-s and enlightened beings, this light extends much more, and with a little focus, even an average sādhak can easily see this.

Ultra-weak photon emissions

A 2014 study by modern scientists has shown that there are very weak photon emissions from living systems that have been termed ultra-weak photon emissions (UPE). They found that biological systems continuously emit very weak light without any external stimuli. This phenomenon, currently commonly termed ultra-weak photon emission, is interesting even more because it was found to be present virtually in all metabolically active systems from the level of bacteria, fungi, germinating seeds, whole plants, animal tissue cultures and whole organisms, including human beings.[44] This finding is significant as it points to a biological understanding of aura.

So, why can't most of us see the aura?

According to another study conducted in 2009 by Japanese researchers, they found that the intensity of the light emitted by the human body is 1000 times lower than the sensitivity of our naked eyes. They said that 'human bioluminescence in visible light exists - it's just too dim for our weak eyes to pick up on.' The study defines bioluminescence as 'the result of highly reactive free radicals produced through cell respiration interacting with free-floating lipids and proteins.'[45] This is why the light of the aura is not easily perceived by ordinary humans. However, those who are sensitive enough to

---

44 Michal Cifra, Pavel Pospíšil. Ultra-weak photon emission from biological samples: Definition, mechanisms, properties, detection and applications, Journal of Photochemistry and Photobiology B: Biology, Volume 139, 2014, Pages 2-10, ISSN 1011-1344, https://doi.org/10.1016/j.jphotobiol.2014.02.009.

45 Kobayashi M, Kikuchi D, Okamura H. Imaging of ultraweak spontaneous photon emission from human body displaying diurnal rhythm. PLoS One. 2009 Jul 16;4(7):e6256. doi: 10.1371/journal.pone.0006256. PMID: 19606225; PMCID: PMC2707605.

perceive it will see how an increase in the frequency of vibration owing to a sudden rush of emotions or any spiritual practice such as chanting, meditating, etc., will increase the intensity of the aura, making it more easily visible.

Those who are clairvoyant will be able to see more than just light. They will be able to see colours in this light of the aura. Light, after all, is composed of colours.

While the Eastern masters did not openly talk about it, the Western clairvoyants have written extensively about it. We find these accounts in the books written by Joseph Ostrom, Annie Besant and C.W. Leadbeater, to name a few. Their books provide confirmation of the existence of the colours of the aura and what causes it to change.

Joseph Ostrom, in his book 'You and Your Aura'[46] defines aura as follows:

> "Aura is a collection of electromagnetic energies of varying densities which are exiting from the physical, vital, etheric, mental, emotional and spiritual bodies. This auric field stands out from the body some 2-3 feet (on average) on all sides. It is also found above the head and extends below the feet into the ground. Another auric field can be found floating above the lower auric field. It can be found anywhere from just at the edge of the lower auric bodies to 50 ft above them. This separate auric field is called the higher auric body."

The work of Joseph Ostrom is important because he had a natural ability to see aura since his childhood. It was what Hindu-s would call a siddhi owing to some pūrva janma saṃskāra (a trait acquired from a previous birth). A point to be noted is that, although Ostrom does not mention it, his description of auric fields finds close coherence with the Hindu understanding of kośa. If kośa is thought of as a sort

---

46 Ostrom, Joseph. 'You and your Aura.' Publication date: 1987

of bio-field surrounding the individual, the aura can be thought of as the light and, consequently, the colour reflected in those fields.

Kośa and aura

According to Ostrom, the first three inner layers of the aura represent aspects pertaining to health and physicality. These layers of the aura are denser and are more easily perceived. The outer two layers are indicators of the emotional and spiritual state of the individual. The outer layers are more subtle and difficult to perceive.

The inner layers can be correlated with the annamaya, prāṇamaya and manōmaya kośa. The outer layers can be correlated to the vijñānamaya and ānandamaya kośa. Those who can read the aura and see its colours will be able to decipher the state of the kośa and thereby know the level (kośa) from which the individual operates.

Below are a few insights from Ostrom's book and their comparison to the knowledge of kośa:

- The first layer, which forms the aura of the physical body (which we can call annamaya kośa), is said to extend only a short distance beyond the skin (3–12 cm), and of all the levels of the aura is the one which the eye can most easily be trained to see. The colours in this aura reflect the state of our physical well-being. Any state of disease will reflect in this aura.

- The second layer of aura (emanating from the prāṇamaya kośa) is said to extend up to 20 cm from the skin. This layer shows the strength of our prāṇa. This level of the aura is responsible for radiating energy from ourselves and also for drawing energy into the cakra-s.

- The third layer of aura relates to the mental sheath (manōmaya kośa) and indicates the mental health of the individual. This aura reveals the emotional state of one's mind.

- The fourth layer of aura represents the higher intelligence (can be said to relate to the vijñānamaya kośa). This layer becomes dominant when one establishes oneself in a higher and subtler reality (such as through yoga and sādhanā). When an individual's awareness rests in this layer, he/she is able to overcome the sway of emotions of the manōmaya kośa and establish oneself in satya (truth) through discriminative knowledge (the knowledge of truth vs untruth). When this layer is strong, the person is highly 'tuned in' to their surroundings and has a high intuitive ability.

- The final kośa is said to be the spiritual sheath described as hovering above the head. We can relate this to the ānandamaya kośa, which speakers of English call the bliss body. The realisation of this kośa occurs when one achieves the final stage of spiritual enlightenment leading to mokṣa. All spiritually realised beings will have a powerful aura emanating from this kośa. Often, the light emanating from deities and Guru-s represented in paintings and photographs is a reference to this aura.

As we become subtle, our aura expands and extends further and further from the centre of our being. Based on the ability of the perceiver, they can see finer divisions within the aura and various hues, tints and shades of each colour. The intensity of the colour and the clarity with which the colour can be seen are all indicators of the subject's physical, emotional and spiritual state.

Back in 1939, an attempt was made to photographically capture the aura through a method known as Kirlian photography, named after the Russian scientist who discovered it. Kirlian discovered that if an object on a photographic plate is subjected to a high-voltage electric field, an image is created on the plate. The image looks like a coloured halo or a coronal discharge. This image is said to be the physical manifestation of the electromagnetic radiation around the body (aura), which is said to surround everything.

Western clairvoyants and mystics were able to perceive the subtle light of the aura, see the colours in it and even comprehend that the colours were the results of the thoughts and emotions of the individuals emitting it. The enlightened ṛṣi-s of Bhārat not only knew all of this several thousand years ago but also devised a system of living based on a deeper understanding of aura. This system is the Varṇa Dharma.

The understanding of varṇa as aura and the classification of society based on it is intended to facilitate every individual to fulfil the purpose of human birth, which is to work towards mokṣa. If we realise this, we will realise that the dharma śāstra texts, which are based on varṇa dharma, are, in fact, mokṣa śāstra-s.

Connecting varṇa to colour

The most popular understanding of varṇa is based on guṇa and karma, as given in the Bhagvad Gītā (Chapter 18, verses 42 to 44). Guṇa (characteristic or quality) and karma (action) are the external manifestations of a subtle change happening within the individual. For individuals who are incapable of sensing subtle phenomena such as aura, the enlightened masters pointed out these external factors, which can be used as indicators of varṇa.

Let us now connect the missing pieces in the definitions of varṇa and the manifested qualities of guṇa and karma to understand what the ṛṣi-s said.

In the dharmaśāstra definitions of varṇa, we see that each varṇa is correlated to different parts of the body of the divine Puruṣa, as given in the ṚgVeda's Puruṣa Sūkta[47] and reiterated by Manu. The Jaiminīya Brāhmaṇa (1.68-9) gives a similar definition of varṇa as that of the Puruṣa Sūkta, but adds the stomach and reproductive organs as the

---

47 ṚgVeda 10.90.12 - ब्राह्मणोऽस्य मुखमासीद्बाहू राजन्यः कृतः । ऊरू तदस्य यद्वैश्यः पद्भ्यां शूद्रो अजायत ॥ "His mouth became the Brāhmaṇa, his arms became the Rājanya, his thighs became the Vaiśya; the Śūdra was born from his feet."

seat of origin of the vaiśya varṇa. We also see that there is a specific guṇa and karma associated with each varṇa, as given in the Bhagvad Gītā and Śrīmad Bhāgavatam. This can be summarised in the table below as the starting point of the creation of varṇa and the resulting external manifestation of varṇa.

Table 1: Origin and manifestation of varṇa

Puruṣa Sūkta creation of varṇa	?	?	Guṇa-Karma manifestation of varṇa from the Bhagvad Gītā & Śrīmad Bhāgavatam
Brāhmaṇa from the mouth			śamaḥ—tranquillity, arising out of the control of the internal organs (like mind), damaḥ - restraint i.e. control of external organs and senses, tapaḥ - austerity, śaucam - purity, kṣhāntiḥ - patience, ārjavam – integrity and honesty, jñānam - knowledge (by reading scriptures), vijñānam - wisdom gained through the experience of applying the knowledge, and āstikyam - faith (in scriptures, God etc.).
Kṣatriya from the arms			śauryaṁ - valour/heroism, tejaḥ - strength, dhṛitiḥ - fortitude/perseverance, dākṣhyaṁ yuddhe - skill in weaponry/battle, cha api apalāyanam - not retreating from battle, dānam - generosity, īśhvara bhāvaḥ - leadership quality, kṣhātram—of the warrior and administrative class

Puruṣa Sūkta creation of varṇa	?	?	Guṇa-Karma manifestation of varṇa from the Bhagvad Gītā & Śrīmad Bhāgavatam
Vaiśya from the thighs, reproductive organs and stomach*			āstikyam – faith in God, dāna-niṣṭhā – charity, adambhaḥ - humility, brahma-sevanam – service unto the brāhmaṇa-s, atuṣṭiḥ arthopacayair – an insatiety from the amassing of wealth**
Śūdra from the feet			śuśrūṣaṇaṁ dvija gavāṁ devānām - service to brāhmaṇa-s, cows, demigods, tatra labdhena santoṣaḥ - complete satisfaction with whatever income is obtained in such service **

Note: *The definition of the vaiśya varṇa is taken from the Puruṣa sūkta (thighs) as well as from Jaiminīya Brāhmaṇa (reproductive organs and stomach).

**The description of guṇa-karma for vaiśya and śūdra varṇa is taken from Śrīmad Bhāgavatam since it is more descriptive than the Bhagvad Gītā.

The seeming lack of connection between the first and the last column of the above table is the puzzle which we need to solve. The missing columns in between are the pieces that connect the origin of varṇa and the external manifestation of varṇa. We shall now attempt to fill in the missing links.

The definition of varṇa as per the Puruṣa Sūkta correlates beautifully to the regions of the dominance of the pañcamahābhūta-s (five elements) in our body. This is mentioned in the Yogōpaniṣad text titled Tri-śikhi-Brahmanōpaniṣad, as given below:

1. From the knee down to the sole of the foot is the seat of pṛthvi (earth element)

2. From the knee up to the hip is said to be the seat of jalā/ varuṇā (water element)

3. From the middle of the body down to the hip is said to be the seat of agni (fire element)

4. From the navel upwards to the nose is the seat of the vāyu (air element)

5. From the nose up to the cavern of the Brahman is the seat of ākāśa (ether element)

Thus, the śūdra varṇa can be said to have the dominant qualities of pṛthvi tattva, vaiśya varṇa of jalā and agni, kṣatriya varṇa of agni and vāyu tattva, and brāhmaṇa varṇa of vāyu and ākāśa tattva.

Next, each of the pañcamahābhūta-s can be correlated to specific cakra-s[48] in the sūkṣma śarīra (subtle body). Ancient tantric texts such as the Ṣaṭ-Cakra-Nirūpaṇa by Paramahaṃsa Swami Pūrṇānanda,[49] as well as some of the Yogōpaniṣad texts, describe each cakra as corresponding to a specific pañcamahābhūta, having a specific colour and a set of specific guṇa-s. Upon comparison, we will find that the guṇa-s specified for each varṇa correlates to the cakra corresponding to that guṇa. Thus, we can say that each of the varṇa-s also corresponds to specific cakra-s.

Cakra-s are known to vibrate at specific frequencies, with the lowest cakra having the lowest frequency and the highest cakra having the highest frequency of vibration corresponding to colours in the visible spectrum of light. These frequencies are not random but instead

---

48 Cakra-s are junctions in the subtle anatomy, where several subtle channels (nādi-s) that carry prāṇa (subtle life force), meet and branch out. The previous books by the same author can be studied for more information on cakra-s.

49 Ṣaṭ Cakra Nirūpaṇa is a text written by Paramahaṃsa Swami Pūrṇānanda, a celebrated Tantric scholar of the 16th century. What he recorded in the book is what he actually visualized through the blessings of his Guru.

correspond to the frequencies of the colours of the rainbow, which we refer to as VIBGYOR. Thus, each cakra is often represented as one of the VIBGYOR colours, with red being associated with the lowest frequency of Mūlādhāra, orange with Svādhiṣṭhāna, yellow with Manipūra, green with Anāhata; blues, indigoes and violets are often correlated with varying frequencies of the Viśuddhi, and white which is the combination of all colours arises from the high frequency of the Ājña cakra.

Thus, we have actual colours (in the aura) for each varṇa, based on the cakra from which that varṇa naturally operates, making the meaning of varṇa as colour come alive. We see this correlation brought out in the table below, filling in the missing pieces of Table 1.

Table 2: Pañcabhūta-s, cakra-s and varṇa correlation

Puruṣa Sūkta creation of varṇa	Dominant Pañca-bhūta of each varṇa	Cakra & colours of each varṇa	Guṇa-Karma from Bhagvad Gītā & Śrīmad Bhāgavatam
Brāhmaṇa from mouth	vāyu and ākāśa	Anāhata (green), Viśuddhi (blues), Ājña & Sahasrāra (white, i.e. all colours)	śamaḥ, damaḥ, tapaḥ, śaucham, kṣhāntiḥ, ārjavam, jñānam, vijñānam, āstikyam
Kṣatriya from arms	vāyu and agni	Viśuddhi (blues, indigoes, violets) & Anāhata (greens). Also, Manipūra for agni (yellow)	śauryaṁ, tejaḥ, dhṛitiḥ, dākṣhyaṁ yuddhe, cha api apalāyanam, dānam, īśhvara bhāvaḥ, kṣhātram
Vaiśya from thighs, reproductive organs & stomach	jalā and agni	Svādhiṣṭhāna (orange) and Manipura for agni (yellow)	āstikyam, dāna-niṣṭhā, adambhaḥ, brahma-sevanam, atuṣṭiḥ arthopacayair

Puruṣa Sūkta creation of varṇa	Dominant Pañca-bhūta of each varṇa	Cakra & colours of each varṇa	Guṇa-Karma from Bhagvad Gītā & Śrīmad Bhāgavatam
Śūdra from feet	Pṛthvi	Mūlādhāra (red)	śuśrūṣaṇaṁ dvija gavāṁ devānām/ paricaryā

Note that the reason why women (of menstrual age) have many of the rules similar to that of the śūdra varṇa is due to the dominance of the qualities of mūlādhāra and svādhiṣṭhāna cakra during their menstrual years.

Clairvoyants like Ostrom and Besant say that the colours seen in the aura are rarely of a single distinct shade. Based on the change in emotions, the shades of the colours, which are due to the varying intensities of light, will vary. In the book 'Thought Forms', Annie Besant presented coloured sketches of the changes in the auric field, which she observed as the thoughts and emotions of the subjects under observation changed. The description of different shades of colours seen in the aura is also described beautifully by Joseph Ostrom, based on his observation of several subjects whose auric fields he used to sketch upon request.

In Table 3, to the descriptions of colour, as seen and described by Ostrom and Besant, we have an added column mentioning the cakra to make the correlation easier. For each colour, the wavelength is also given. Do note that wavelength is inversely proportional to frequency, which means that for longer wavelength waves (such as red), the frequency of vibration will be the lowest, and for shorter wavelength waves (such as blue), the frequency of vibration will be higher. As we go from red (mūlādhāra) to white (ājña), the wavelength keeps reducing, and the frequency of vibration keeps increasing.

Table 3: Colour, emotion and cakra correlation

Colour & wavelength	Emotions	Cakra
Reds 740–625 nm	Red is the colour of physical activity. It is a low-vibration colour representing animal nature, sense experience and all things based on physical and materialistic thinking. On the negative side, certain reds can indicate anger, selfishness, hate, and even murder. Other muddy shades of red indicate lust and base sexual desire. When love manifests as unselfish and unconditional affection, free from attachment, red becomes a soft pink.	Mūlādhāra cakra
Oranges 625–590 nm	Orange is a balanced mixture of red (physical) and yellow (mental) activity. Psychologically, orange generates wakefulness and activity. The activity is one of constant balancing and harmonising. Orange in the aura indicates a period of transition, healing and growth. If it does not transition to greens, it indicates a sort of repression of emotions and takes a muddy hue. Note: For Hindu-s, orange is also the colour of sanyās (withdrawal of reproductive process of Svādhiṣṭhāna cakra). In this case, there is a conscious repression of emotions associated with this cakra, such as kāma, krodha, etc., for pursuing the spiritual path of a renunciate.	Svādhiṣṭhāna cakra (and also Mūlādhāra or Manipūra based on the shade)

Colour & wavelength	Emotions	Cakra
Yellows 590–565 nm	All yellows are representative of intellect and mental activity. Each shade or tint of yellow is said to express a type of functioning ability or expression of the intellect, from the craftiness of the mustard yellow to the high thought of a light yellow to the timidity represented by a ruddy yellow.	Manipūra cakra
Greens 565–520 nm	Green is the colour of growth and renewal. In the aura, the presence of clear, bright grass-green is a positive sign, which suggests that the storm has passed and growth and renewal processes are happening. On the other hand, people who are envious or jealous will display an ugly, muddy, dark green in the aura (hence the phrase 'green with envy').	Anāhata cakra
Blues Cyan: 520–500 nm Blue: 500–435 nm Violet: 435–380 nm	There are blues that represent the highest intuitive ability (such as indigo) and blues that represent the deepest of melancholia. All colours in the blue group represent the connection of an informational process to the brain. Dark blues are cooling and soothing. Sky blue indicates that the emotional health of the individual is at its most positive. Indigo and violet represent the intuitive and spiritual in combination.	Viśuddhi cakra is traditionally associated with blue. Ājña cakra is considered vibrationally connected to this colour, and it is a good stimulator for it. Shades of violet, such as lavender, are also associated with Sahasrāra cakra.

Colour & wavelength	Emotions	Cakra
White (consists of wavelengths of all colours ranging from 400 – 700 nm)	White has the highest vibration and is considered a protective colour. It indicates purity of spirit and the absolute presence of light. Note: Buddhists consider white to be the highest in terms of vibration, the second being gold, while violet is considered to be the third highest.	Ājña cakra

Note: nm refers to nanometre, which in SI units is 1×10^{-9} metres (m)

Thus, we see the connection between emotions, colours and varṇa, through the correlation of the frequency of vibration of different cakra-s.

Interestingly, the Nāṭyaśāstra text, which has details of Bhārat's traditional dramatic arts, dance and music, provides a description of colours for different emotions or sentiments called rasa, as given below (from Chapter VI - Rasādhyaḥ):[50]

श्यामो भवेत्तु शृङ्गारः सितो हास्यः प्रकीर्तितः ।

कपोतः करुणश्चैव रक्तो रौद्रः प्रकीर्तितः - ॥42॥

गौरो वीरस्तु विज्ञेयः कृष्णश्चापि भयानकः।

नीलवर्णस्तु बीभत्सः पीतश्चैवाद्भुतः स्मृतः - ॥43॥

śṛṅgāra (erotic sentiment) is śyāma (greens or blues), hāsya (comic sentiment) is sita (white), karuna (pathos) is kapota (grey), raudra (anger) is rakta (red), vīra (heroism) is gaura (yellowish-red), bhayānaka (dreadful) is kṛṣṇa (black),

---

50 Nāṭyaśāstram, ascribed to Bharata Muni, translated by Manomohan Ghosh. Chaukhamba Subraharati Prakashan. Volume 1.

bibhitsā (odious) is nīla (blue), and adbhuta (wonder) is pīta (yellow).[51]

In the same Nāṭyaśāstra text, in the section on cosmetics and makeup, there are descriptions of how male actors should paint their limbs based on the characters they are depicting. In this section, we find a direct mention of the colours to be painted by those portraying characters of different varṇa (Chapter XXIII - āhāryābhinayaḥ):[52]

ब्राह्मणाः क्षत्रियाश्चैव गौराः कार्याः सदैव हि ।।107।।

वैश्याः शूद्रास्तथा चैव श्यामाः कार्यास्तु वर्णतः।

Brāhmaṇa and kṣatriya should be represented by gaura (obtained by mixing red and yellow), while vaiśya and śūdra should be śyāma (greenish blue or bluish green).

A similar instruction is given for the type of preferred clothing for each varṇa in Āpastamba Dharmasūtra as well. Understanding this reveals a very nuanced knowledge of colours known to the ancient seers. Unlike emotions which directly alter one's vibration showing the colour corresponding to the emotion (rasa) in the aura, when one's body is painted or covered with clothes of a particular colour, it means that the person has reflected that colour which is seen and has absorbed all the other colours.

---

51 śṛṅgāra is an elevated form of kāma; while kāma operates from the lower cakra-s, śṛṅgāra is from anāhata (heart) and hence is of śyāma varṇa. In case of hāsya, it is divided into six types such as slight smile (smita), smile (hasita), gentle laughter (vihasita), laughter of ridicule (upahasita), vulgur laughter (apahasita) and excessive laughter (atihasita). The first two belong to the superior, the next two middling and the last two to inferior category. White is the colour which contains all other colours, and hence it makes sense that hasya is assigned white given the number of varieties of hāsya. In case of bibhitsa, the exact meaning is 'desire to break through' which corresponds to the viśuddhi cakra and hence blue makes sense. The others sentiments and colours assigned are self-explanatory.

52 Nāṭyaśāstram, ascribed to Bharata Muni, translated by Manomohan Ghosh. Chaukhamba Subraharati Prakashan. Volume 1.

In the modern understanding of colour, we understand that the colour we see is the wavelength of light that it reflects while absorbing all other wavelengths. So, when an artist depicting a brāhmaṇa or a kṣatriya paints themself in the gaura colour, it means that they absorb all the other higher wavelength colours which show in their aura (while reflecting lower wavelengths of red to yellow). Similarly, when they play the character of a vaiśya or śūdra and paint themselves in the śyāma colour, it means they absorb all the other lower wavelength colours which show in their aura (while reflecting higher wavelengths of greens to blues). Thus, the character artist's aura temporarily shows the colours of the varṇa which they portray. In Nāṭyaśāstra, much care is taken to ensure that the artist gets into the skin of the character and temporarily becomes the character that he depicts. This perfection is ensured even to the subtlest level of the aura of the character by using appropriate colours. Thus, we see a highly nuanced, scientific understanding of varṇa, even in places where we least expect it.

Sometimes, the same knowledge is also shared as simple stories. One such story, which is yet more evidence of the knowledge of aura and its connection to varṇa is shared below.

The description of aura as light (jyotiḥ) can be seen in a story from the Chāndogya Upaniṣad (Kanda 4, section 1 onwards), which speaks about the king Jānaśruti who undertook a lot of charitable work, but later felt dejected that he did not attain real wisdom, and begs the sage Raikva to teach him. In two verses of this story (4.1.2 and 4.2.3), we see the recognition of the aura of King Jānaśruti. The first time, it is mentioned as a bright light that has spread over the sky like daylight when swans see him as they fly above. Later, when the swans tease that his aura is not comparable to that of the great sage Raikva, the king feels dejected and goes looking for Raikva. When the king finally meets the sage, he tries to incentivise him by offering him wealth and then asks the sage to teach him. But the sage looks at Jānaśruti and calls him a śūdra, meaning the king is feeling so sorrowful that his aura has become that of a śūdra, losing its earlier light as seen by the swans. The sage Raikva, who could clearly see this, refused to teach him. The two verses are given below:

अथ हंसा निशायामतिपेतुस्तद्धैवं हं सोहं समभ्युवाद हो होऽयि भल्लाक्ष भल्लाक्ष जानश्रुतेः पौत्रायणस्य समं दिवा ज्योतिराततं तन्मा प्रसाङ्क्षी स्तत्त्वा मा प्रधाक्षीरिति ॥ ४.१.२ ॥

The swan flying behind called out to the one ahead: 'Hey, you short-sided one! Don't you see that the brightness of Jānaśruti (his aura) has spread all over the sky like daylight? Beware, you don't touch it. See that it doesn't burn you.' Here, the use of 'jānaśruteḥ pautrāyaṇasya jyotiḥ' the light [emanating] from Jānaśruti, the great-grandson of Janaśruta, is a reference to his aura.

तमु ह परः प्रत्युवाचाह हारेत्वा शूद्र तवैव सह गोभिरस्त्विति तदु ह पुनरेव जानश्रुतिः पौत्रायणः सहस्रं गवां निष्कमश्वतरीरथं दुहितरं तदादाय प्रतिचक्रमे ॥ ४.२.३ ॥

Raikva said to him, 'You śūdra, the necklace and chariot along with the cows—let all these be yours.' Jānaśruti left and then again came back—this time with one thousand cows, a gold necklace, a chariot drawn by mules, and his own daughter.

The sage Raikva could sense the change in the colour of Jānaśruti's aura and responded according to what he saw (a śūdra) rather than the known status of Jānaśruti (a kṣatriya) by examining his aura.

The Chāndogya Upaniṣad also mentions something fascinating that might help us decode the basis of the changes reflected in the colours of the aura. While the Western clairvoyants wrote their observation of the different shades, tints and hues of colours as seen in the aura,[53] a subtle understanding is provided in the Chāndogya Upaniṣad regarding what causes these shades, tints and hues to

---

53 Hues, Shades, Tints: In general as per modern knowledge, the blending of the Primary Colors (Red, Blue and Yellow) in varied proportions produce what is known as the 'hues' of colour. Adding white to the hues, we obtain 'tints', while mixing black produces 'shades.' Source: 'The Human Aura' by Swami Panchadasi

occur. From verses 6.4.1 onwards, there is a description of three fundamental colours – rohita (red), śukla (white) and kṛṣṇa (black). Consider the below verses in the Chāndogya Upaniṣad:

एतद्ध स्म वै तद्विद्वांस आहुः पूर्वं महाशाला महाश्रोत्रिया न नोऽद्य कश्चनाश्रुतममतमविज्ञातमुदाहरिष्यतीति ह्येभ्यो विदांचक्रुः ॥ ६.४.५ ॥

"The earlier great householders, who were well read in the Veda-s, knew this. They said, 'There is nothing anyone can mention that is not heard of or thought of or already known to us.' This is because they came to know about the three colours." – 6.4.5

यदु रोहितमिवाभूदिति तेजसस्तद्रूपमिति तद्विदांचक्रुर्यदु शुक्लमिवाभूदित्यपांरूपमिति तद्विदांचक्रुर्यदु कृष्णमिवाभूदित्यन्नस्य रूपमिति तद्विदांचक्रुः ॥ ६.४.६ ॥

"They knew that whatever else was seen as red was the colour of fire; whatever else was seen as white was the colour of water; and whatever else was seen as dark was the colour of earth." - 6.4.6

यद्वविज्ञातमिवाभूदित्येतासामेव देवतानांसमास इति तद्विदांचक्रुर्यथा तु खलु सोम्येमास्तिस्रो देवताः पुरुषं प्राप्य त्रिवृत्त्रिवृदेकैका भवति तन्मे विजानीहीति ॥ ६.४.७ ॥

"And whatever else was not properly known they understood was the combination of those three deities [fire, water, and earth]. O Somya (son), now learn from me how these three deities enter into a person and become threefold." – 6.4.7

According to Āyurveda, the fire element is predominantly made up of sattva and rajoguṇa-s, the water element is made up of sattva and tamoguṇa, while the earth element is predominantly made up of tamoguṇa.[54] Therefore, when one's personality has the qualities

---

54 Sattva, Rajas and Tamas are the three guṇa-s. Sattva is the principle of inherent intelligence and consciousness in the universe, Rajas is the creative energy and the motive principle in the universe, Tamas is the principle

of sattva and rajas, there could be hues of red mixed in the colours of the aura. Similarly, when one's personality has sattva and tamas, there could be tints of white in the aura making it look bright. And when one's personality has the tamoguṇa as the main quality, there could be blackish shades in the aura. This means that based on the three guṇa-s and the dominance of each at any given time, the natural colours of one's aura could have a reddish, whitish or blackish appearance.

Thus, we find that the ṛṣi-s had a very fine understanding of aura, its variations and even the subtle reasons that caused it to vary. The Chāndogya Upaniṣad says that those who know this are considered as having known all there is to know.

Anumāna & Upamāna Pramāṇa

So far, we have used the inference method called anumāna and the comparison method called upamāna to arrive at the correlation of varṇa to kośa-s, bhūta-s, cakra-s and guṇa-s. We will now elaborately describe these interconnections, taking the guṇa-karma definitions from the Bhagavad Gītā as a foundation.

In the 18th chapter of the Bhagavad Gītā, from verses 42 to 44, Śrī Kṛṣṇa describes different varṇa-s on the basis of karma (activity) and guṇa (quality).[55] A few verses from Śrīmad Bhāgavatam have also been added for a clearer understanding of the guṇa-s of the vaiśya and śūdra varṇa, since these are not elaborated in the Gītā. In the paragraphs that follow, we compare and correlate these guṇa-s and karma-s attributed to each varṇa with the corresponding kośa, cakra and aura colours.

---

of nescience/illusion and also indicates inertia or rest. Suśruta Saṃhita (Sūtrasthānam Chapter XXIV) says that the three guṇa-s are inherent in and inseparable from all the phenomenal appearances in the universe.

55 Source for the word-to-word definition is https://www.holy-bhagavad-gita.org/

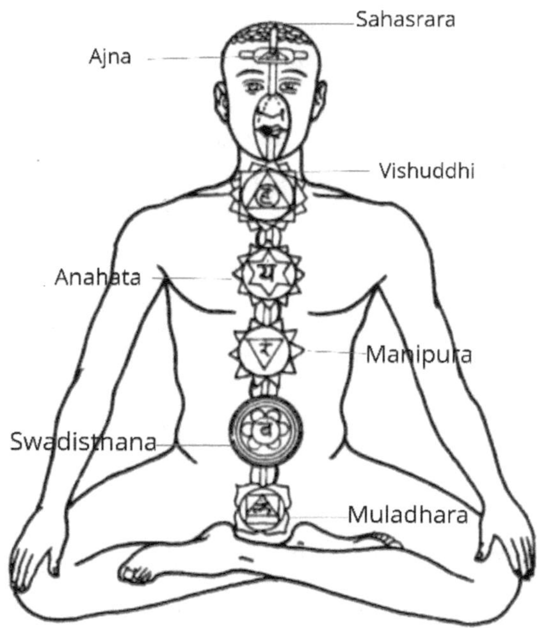

Fig 1. Location of cakra-s (Source: Swami Sivananda, Kundalini Yoga, 1994)

Brāhmaṇa varṇa (chapter 18, sloka 42):

शमो दमस्तप: शौचं क्षान्तिरार्जवमेव च |

ज्ञानं विज्ञानमास्तिक्यं ब्रह्मकर्म स्वभावजम् || 42||

śamo damas tapaḥ śaucaṁ kṣāntir ārjavam eva ca

jñānaṁ vijñānam āstikyaṁ brahma-karma svabhāva-jam

The natural duties/tendencies of the brāhmaṇa varṇa are śamaḥ—tranquillity, arising out of the control of the internal organs (like mind), damaḥ - restraint, i.e. control of external organs and senses, tapaḥ - austerity, śaucam - purity (of mind, body and actions), kṣāntiḥ - patience, ārjavam - integrity and honesty, jñānam - knowledge (by reading scriptures), vijñānam - wisdom gained through the experience of applying the knowledge, and āstikyam - faith (in scriptures and God).

Kośa: In the guṇa described for the brāhmaṇa varṇa, we see that the vijñānamaya kośa is very dominant, with the chance of resting awareness in the ānandamaya kośa being a possibility. The control of the mind and sense organs can only happen for one whose awareness is thoroughly established in the vijñānamaya kośa. The knowledge of the scriptures and the wisdom gained by applying this knowledge opens the possibility of taking awareness to the ānandamaya kośa.

Cakra: The quality of vijñānam corresponds to the viśuddhi and that of āstikyam to the anāhata. Further, true jñānam can only happen when one is able to connect to the divine source of knowledge. Command over the senses and connecting with the higher realities through the Guru's anugraha are possible through the ājña cakra. Once this is established, the possibility of experiencing samādhi avasthā and the opening of the sahasrāra cakra is a possibility for the brāhmaṇa varṇa.

Colours: The colours of the anāhata are green, that of the viśuddhi cakra are the shades of blue and white is the colour of the ājña cakra. These are the colours that would show in the kośa and thereby in the aura of the brāhmaṇa varṇa, if he followed his svadharma and also based on which of the guṇa-s are predominant at any given time.

Kṣatriya varṇa (chapter 18, sloka 43):

शौर्यं तेजो धृतिर्दाक्ष्यं युद्धे चाप्यपलायनम् ।

दानमीश्वरभावश्च क्षात्रं कर्म स्वभावजम् ॥ 43॥

śauryaṁ tejo dhṛitir dākṣyaṁ yuddhe cāpy apalāyanam

dānam īśvara-bhāvaś ca kṣātraṁ karma svabhāva-jam

The natural duties/tendencies of the kṣatriya varṇa are śauryaṁ - valour/heroism, tejaḥ - strength, dhṛitiḥ - fortitude/perseverance, dākṣyaṁ yuddhe - skill in weaponry/battle, ca api apalāyanam - not retreating from battle, dānam - generosity, īśvara bhāvaḥ - leadership quality, kṣātram - of the warrior and administrative class.

Kośa: The qualities associated with the mental attitude of valour, fortitude, courage and generosity point to the manōmaya kośa. The skills associated with leadership require one to have the ability to cultivate viveka buddhi (discriminative intelligence), which makes it possible to make tough decisions based on the ability to discern truth from untruth and serve justice. Thus, the awareness will also pertain to vijñānamaya kośa.

Cakra: The firepower to fight battles comes from the manipūra cakra, the generosity of spirit required of a leader from the anāhata cakra and discriminative intelligence from the viśuddhi cakra. After the worldly pursuits of battle and leadership have run their course and the associated prārabda karma has been exhausted, there is a possibility to go up to the ājña cakra if one is strongly established in viśuddhi cakra, and with the blessings of a Guru. Perhaps that is why the term 'Rāja Ṛṣi' exists because a Rāja (king) can also become a Ṛṣi (sage) in his later years.

Colours: The colours in the aura of the kṣatriya varṇa could show a dominance of yellow (manipūra cakra), green (anāhata cakra) and/or blue (viśuddhi cakra), based on which of the guṇa-s are predominant at any given time.

Vaiśya varṇa and Śūdra varṇa (chapter 18, sloka 44)

कृषिगौरक्ष्यवाणिज्यं वैश्यकर्म स्वभावजम् |

परिचर्यात्मकं कर्म शूद्रस्यापि स्वभावजम् || 44||

kṛiṣi-gau-rakṣhya-vāṇijyaṁ vaiśya-karma svabhāva-jam

paricaryātmakaṁ karma śūdrasyāpi svabhāva-jam

The natural duties/tendencies of the vaiśya varṇa are kṛiṣi - agriculture, gau-rakṣhya - protection of cattle (esp. cows)/dairy farming, and vāṇijyam - commerce/business.

The natural duties/tendencies of the śūdra varṇa are paricaryā - duty in the form of service/seva/devotion

As per Śrīmad-Bhāgavatam (11.17.18), the vaiśya varṇa's guṇa-s are described by Śrī Kṛṣṇa as follows:

आस्तिक्यं दाननिष्ठा च अदम्भो ब्रह्मसेवनम् ।

अतुष्टिरर्थोपचयैर्वैश्यप्रकृतयस्त्विमाः ॥ १८ ॥

āstikyaṁ dāna-niṣṭhā ca adambho brahma-sevanam

atuṣṭir arthopacayair vaiśya-prakṛtayas tv imāḥ

The natural tendencies of the vaiśya varṇa are āstikyam - faith in God, dāna-niṣṭhā - charity, adambhaḥ - humility, brahma-sevanam - service unto the brāhmaṇa-s, and atuṣṭiḥ arthopacayair - an insatiety from the amassing of wealth.

Kośa: The creation and maintenance of wealth, working with the earth through agriculture and business acumen can be correlated to the annamaya, prāṇamaya and manōmaya kośa, for the vaiśya varṇa. Faith in God, charity and humility are related to the manōmaya kośa.

Cakra: The svādhiṣṭhāna is the dominant cakra for the vaiśya varṇa, with the possibility of going lower to the mūlādhāra or going higher to the manipūra cakra (especially when it manifests as ambition to gain wealth).

Colours: The colours in the aura of the vaiśya varṇa could show a dominance of orange (svādhiṣṭhāna cakra), shades of reds including pink (mūlādhāra cakra) or yellow (manipūra cakra).

As per Śrīmad-Bhāgavatam (11.17.19), the śūdra varṇa's guṇa-s are described by Śrī Kṛṣṇa as follows:

शुश्रूषणं द्विजगवां देवानां चाप्यमायया ।

तत्र लब्धेन सन्तोष: शूद्रप्रकृतयस्त्विमाः ॥ १९ ॥

śuśrūṣaṇaṁ dvija-gavāṁ devānāṁ cāpy amāyayā

tatra labdhena santoṣaḥ śūdra-prakṛtayas tv imāḥ

The natural tendencies of the śūdra varṇa are śuśrūṣaṇaṁ dvija gavāṁ devānām - service unto the brāhmaṇa-s, cows, demigods and other seva-worthy beings, labdhena santoṣaḥ - complete satisfaction with whatever income is obtained in such service.

Kośa: For the śūdra varṇa, the guṇa prescribed of service to others (seva) is what they need to acquire to overcome the animalistic tendencies of the physical body, failing which there is a high chance that they fall into the category below the four varṇa-s in their next birth. The associated kośa for the śūdra varṇa is predominantly the annamaya kośa and the prāṇamaya kośa, which strongly influences the annamaya kośa.

Cakra: For the śūdra varṇa, the mūlādhāra cakra is the dominant one with a possibility of going higher to the svādhiṣṭhāna cakra.

Colours: The primary colour for the śūdra varṇa's aura would be different shades of red.

Interestingly, in Śrīmad Bhāgavatam (11.17.20), Śrī Kṛṣṇa also talks about the natural tendencies of those who lie beyond the pale of the four varṇa-s, as follows:

अशौचमनृतं स्तेयं नास्तिक्यं शुष्कविग्रह: ।

काम: क्रोधश्च तर्षश्च स भावोऽन्त्यावसायिनाम् ॥ २० ॥

aśaucam anṛtaṁ steyaṁ nāstikyaṁ śuṣka-vigrahaḥ

kāmaḥ krodhaś ca tarṣaś ca sa bhāvo 'ntyāvasāyinām

Lack of cleanliness, falsehood, theft, atheism, useless quarrelling, lust, anger and greed. These are the tendencies of a fifth class beyond the pale of the other four.

Why are seva and bhakti prescribed for the śūdra varṇa?

It is important to contemplate why seva (service to others) and bhakti (devotion) are prescribed as the primary duty of the śūdra varṇa; not the creation of wealth, not battle or leadership and not the pursuit of knowledge, but service to the rest of society and devotion towards the creator. Most people, influenced by the colonial narrative, assume that the reason is to keep the śūdra varṇa in suppression. The colonial narrative went a step further and declared the śāstra as a patriarchal tool devised to use the śūdra varṇa as slaves for the rest of society. This is far from the truth. Whatever applies to the śūdra varṇa applies to every individual who operates from the mūlādhāra cakra and whose aura largely has the colour red, even if it is just a passing phase in their life. And that is why it is crucial to understand how one can overcome this phase by following what the śāstra recommends.

Clairvoyants and healers such as Joseph Ostrom talk about the significance of seeing the colour red in a person's aura. When the person is physically and emotionally healthy, the red reflected is said to be a good, somewhat translucent and bright red. This healthy shade of red, however, is rarely seen, especially in adults. Instead, the red that is mostly seen is a shade that is dark or muddy with the emotions of lust, greed, selfishness, deceit, and other low-frequency emotions.

The colour red has the broadest wavelength and the slowest frequency of vibration compared to the other colours in the visible spectrum. What this means at the atomic level is that when the atoms vibrate at the frequency of red, the electrons occupy the lowest energy shell, which is closest to the nucleus of the atom.[56] Therefore, there is a great pull from the nucleus to keep the electron bound to the atom in its lowest vibrating energy shell. For the electron to break free from the pull of the nucleus and to jump to the next higher energy level and thereby change the frequency, colour and resulting aura is no small task, as the force exerted by the nucleus is highest for the electron closest to it. What, then, could free the electron to jump to a higher energy shell? What controls the nucleus and exerts this enormous pull on the electrons? The answer is *the mind.*

---

56 To know more about the behaviour of electrons in an atom, one may study Bohr's model of Hydrogen atom and Electron Transition series.

German physicist Max Planck said,

> "I can tell you as a result of my research about atoms this much: There is no matter as such. All matter originates and exists only by virtue of a force which brings the particle of an atom to vibration and holds this most minute solar system of the atom together. We must assume behind this force the existence of a conscious and intelligent mind. This mind is the matrix of all matter."

Quantum physicists call this conscious and intelligent mind the Quantum Field. In the book 'Becoming Supernatural', Dr. Joe Dispenza explains that 'our thoughts are electric, our emotions are magnetic, and together they make an electromagnetic field around our body. Our electromagnetic field is always communicating with the quantum field. If we change our electromagnetic field (by changing our thoughts and emotions), then that will attract a new reality from the quantum field. The thought must match the feeling, and then we have to hold that state of being long enough for the manifestation to occur.'

Similarly, if we understand what the ṛṣi-s of Bhārat have been saying, the answer for the well-being of one who operates from the lowest energy level of an atom (the śūdra varṇa) is to loosen the mind by letting go of 'aham' or I-centredness.

Aham is that which keeps one from progressing in the spiritual path. No matter which varṇa one belongs to, overcoming self-centred thoughts and actions is a must to progress spiritually. Therefore, the practice of dānam and generosity is a must for the first three varṇa-s (brāhmaṇa, kṣatriya and vaiśya). The śūdra varṇa, on the other hand, is not expected to hand over their wealth to the government (as tax) or to others as dānam, as per the śāstra-s. The ṛṣi-s understood that the jivātma whose journey is in the śūdra phase, has other concerns which keep them preoccupied.

Aham is not just ego or ego-centric behaviour as translated by speakers of the English language. In this context, aham also refers to an excessive concern about oneself, to the exclusion of everyone and everything else. It is the mind of a person who is unable to (due to personal problems) or does not wish to (owing to selfishness) think for anyone other than himself/herself.

When red is the dominant colour in one's aura, the mūlādhāra cakra is the seat of thought and action. Mūlādhāra cakra, when weak due to insufficient prāṇa, causes the individual to experience feelings of fear, insecurity, self-doubt, poor health, fertility issues and financial difficulties. Such a person is so caught up in trying to just stay afloat that it becomes very difficult for them to think for others (and thus overcome aham-ness.)

If Mūlādhāra is overly active with more prāṇa than it can handle or be channelised safely, then the individual might exhibit deviant social behaviour such as addiction to porn, drugs, animalistic tendencies, desire to murder, and a craving for all excesses. The strong aham keeps the individual addicted to gross animalistic needs and desires without caring about consequences.

By cultivating an attitude of seva towards others, the disturbed red aura of lust and desire can transform into a beautiful light pink aura of compassion and selfless love towards others. By practising bhakti and surrendering to the divine, the fear of doing wrong keeps one from falling low and succumbing towards animalistic and dangerous behaviour. Thus, seva is recommended as a means of gently altering the thought vibrations for the śūdra varṇa.

This understanding is why the popular verse given below describes the śūdra varṇa as one who is śocanīya, that is, one who is in a woeful, deplorable, sorrowful state, and for whom paricaryā or service to others is considered as svadharma as a means to lift himself out of that low state.

"ब्रह्म ज्ञानेन ब्राह्मणः

क्षतात् रक्षति इति क्षत्रियः

व्यापार व्यवहारेषु वेशनेन वैश्यः

शोचन्तंश्च परिचर्यासु ये रताः ते शूद्राः"

"One who has the knowledge of Brahma is brāhmaṇa; one who protects is the kṣatriya; one who is engaged in trade and business is the vaiśya; the sorrowful one for whom paricaryā (seva) is the recommended path, is the śūdra."

When the mind is at its absolute lowest, the mental effort that can pull the individual out of the web of sorrow is the practice of seva and bhakti. Next time you feel depressed or any other negative emotion, try doing an act of seva for someone else or surrender to the divine, and experience how it can transform the way you feel, even in the short term. If one can practice both seva and bhakti, then the negativity in life will disappear, and one will automatically move to the next level of emotional, material and spiritual progress.

Can varṇa change if we change the guṇa-karma?

While the Puruṣa Sūkta and the Triśikhi Brahmanopaniṣad seem rather specific about the region of operation of each varṇa and pañcabhūta within the body, the description of guṇa and karma in the Gītā indicates a possibility of going either up or down one or more cakra-s for each varṇa, in each birth. Each birth is, therefore, a possibility to climb up one or more steps from one's inherent varṇa by following dharma or fall down one or more steps through adharma. When one reaches fulfilment in each cakra, only then can one go to the next level in a subsequent birth.

A question that might be on the minds of many is if it is possible to change one's varṇa by changing one's behavioural patterns (guṇa) or by forcibly causing oneself to operate from the higher cakra-s by chanting mantra-s or performance of action (karma) meant for a higher varṇa. In other words, is varṇa birth-based or behaviour-based?

The birth-based definition of varṇa applies to a person who belongs to a particular varṇa by birth, i.e., if born in lawful wedlock of parents, both of whom belong to that varṇa.[57] This is stated in Manu, Yājñavalkya, Viṣṇu Dharmasūtra and many other texts, as given below:

Manu (X.10.5) says:

सर्ववर्णेषु तुल्यासु पत्नीष्वक्षततयोनिषु ।

आनुलोम्येन सम्भूता जात्या ज्ञेयास्त एव ते ॥ ५ ॥

'Among all varṇa-s, those only who are born of consorts wedded in the natural order, as virgins of equal status, are to be regarded as the same (as their father).'—(5)

Yājñavalkya (I.90) says:

सवर्णेभ्यः सवर्णासु जायन्ते हि सजातयः ।

अनिन्द्येषु विवाहेषु पुत्राः संतानवर्धनाः ॥

'By men of the same varṇa in women of the same varṇa are born sajāti (sons of equal birth or varṇa). In blameless marriages, sons (are begotten) continuing the line.'

Viṣṇu Dharmasūtra 16.1 says:

समानवर्णासु पुत्राः सवर्णा भवन्ति १

'On women equal in varṇa (to their husbands), sons are begotten, who are equal in varṇa (to their fathers).'

---

57 Note that the śāstra-s reiterate that it must be a lawful wedlock, failing which even though both parents are of the same varṇa, the child will not be considered so. This is due to the rituals undertaken during the vivāha saṃskāra, which bring the bride and groom in alignment with each other, thereby causing the progeny to be of the proper energetic combination of the two.

The reason for this is that only when both parents carry the same frequency of vibration can the child naturally have that frequency of vibration in his physical body. The performance of karma and the practice of guṇa-s pertaining to that varṇa will maintain the inherent vibrational quality obtained at birth.

Following the guṇa ascribed to another varṇa, will not result in a change of varṇa acquired at birth; meaning, just by changing the guṇa, one does not become eligible to perform the karma of another varṇa. This is because varṇa is of the physical body, not of the ātma. This is why the Sutāsaṃhita[58] says, 'Varṇa attaches to the body and not to the ātma.' This means that even if one has the guṇa of another, say higher varṇa, their physical body can only handle work up to the vibration with which they were born.

Yes, it is true that a few texts, such as Śāntiparva (189.4 & 8), mention that varṇa is to be recognised by guṇa and not by birth. These statements were made in the context of people only relying on birth and not bothering to keep up with the guṇa-karma prescribed for the given varṇa. So if one who is a brāhmaṇa by virtue of birth indulges in kāma, krodha, etc., naturally his vibrations will alter, and he will not be fit for performing the karma of a brāhmaṇa until he aligns his mind with the guṇa-s meant for his varṇa. But on the other hand, even if a śūdra overcomes the pull of the lower tendencies and practices great restraint, bhakti and other characteristics of a brāhmaṇa, he does modify his guṇa through mental effort, but his physical body will still not be able to handle the karma of a brāhmaṇa.

Yes, one's modified guṇa will get stored as subtle vibrations in the kāraṇa śarīra (causal body) and cause a corresponding change in the

---

58 पश्वादीनां यथा जातिर्जन्मनैव न चान्यथा ॥ ५१ ॥ साऽपि स्थूलस्य देहस्य भौतिकस्य न चाऽस्त्मनः । तथाऽपि देहेऽहंमानादात्मा विप्रादिसंज्ञितः ॥ ५२ ॥ - Suta Samhita Śivamāhātmyakhanda (12:51 & 52)

varṇa as per guṇa, but only in the next birth. This is attested by Manu in X.10.42 and others, as given below:

Manu in X.10.42,

तपोबीजप्रभावैस्तु ते गच्छन्ति युगे युगे ।

उत्कर्षं चापकर्षं च मनुष्येष्विह जन्मतः ॥ ४२ ॥

'By the force of austerities and the seed they attain higher or lower rank among men, through birth, cycle after cycle.'—(42)

Āpastamba in (2, 11.10-11)

'In successive births, men of the lower varṇa are born in the next higher one, if they have fulfilled their duties. In successive births, men of the higher varṇa are born in the next lower one, if they have neglected their duties.'

The above verses indicate that when an ātma takes birth as a śūdra for the first time, then it will most likely have to go up the vibration ladder one by one. Hence, a śūdra's ātma is sometimes referred to as a baby-soul, meaning it might be its first time in a human body.[59] So a first-time śūdra might become a vaiśya in the next birth, then a kṣatriya, then a brāhmaṇa if he/she follows the dharmic path and succeeds in each birth to leave the body in a vibrationally higher state of mind. If he/she fails, they will be born in the same or lower vibrational state in the next birth.

However, there are cases of those who were born in a śūdra womb but were known to have the guṇa of a brāhmaṇa. In such cases, it is likely that such an ātma is not a first-time śūdra, meaning it had already been a brāhmaṇa in another birth and, due to the wrong actions, took birth

---

59 Vedanta Sutra of Badarayana, Pada 3, Adhikarana VIII about how śūdra-s are not entitled to Vedic meditation and that śūdra-s get mokṣa through purāṇa-s, and a mukta śūdra is as holy as any other Jiva – Pages 146 to 153 of the series "Sacred Book of Hindus: Vedanta Sutra." Here, it is explained how baby-souls, meaning those who are just coming out of animality into humanity, are not entitled to study Upaniṣads or meditate on Brahman at once.

in a vibrationally lower womb. In such cases, the physical body would have the vibrational ability of the present birth, but the saṃskāra-s would indicate whatever it has learned from previous births. One such story is of a butcher (Dharmavyādha) featured in Mahābhārata, which is covered in detail in the chapter titled 'Exceptions.'

Occupations

Regarding the karma (occupations) allotted for each varṇa - a physical body with a higher frequency of vibration can undertake the work of a lower frequency of vibration, but not the other way around, even if they change their guṇa. This is clearly stated in the dharma śāstra rules regarding the type of occupation to be followed by each varṇa, as given below.

Vasiṣṭha Dharmasūtra (II.22-23) says:

अजीवन्तः स्वधर्मेणानन्तरां यवीयसीं वृत्तिमातिष्ठेरन् २२

न तु कदाचिज्जयायसीम् 23

'Those who are unable to live by their own lawful occupation may adopt (that of) the next inferior (varṇa). But never (that of a) higher (varṇa).'

Manu (X.10.95) says:

जीवेदेतेन राजन्यः सर्वणाप्यनयं गतः ।

न त्वेव ज्यायंसीं वृत्तिमभिमन्येत कर्हि चित् ॥ ९५ ॥

'The kṣatriya, fallen in adverse circumstances, shall subsist by means of all this; but he shall never think of abrogating to himself the higher occupations.'—(95)

Manu (X.10.96) says:

यो लोभादधमो जात्या जीवेदुत्कृष्टकर्मभिः ।

तं राजा निर्धनं कृत्वा क्षिप्रमेव प्रवासयेत् ॥ ९६ ॥

'If a man of low varṇa, through greed, subsists by the occupations of his superiors, the King shall deprive him of his property and quickly banish him.'—(96)

Manu (X.10.97) says:

वरं स्वधर्मो विगुणो न पारक्यः स्वनुष्ठितः ।

परधर्मेण जीवन् हि सद्यः पतति जातितः ॥ ९७ ॥

'Better one's own duty imperfectly performed, and not the duty of another performed perfectly; he who subsists by the function of another, instantly falls off from his varṇa.' — (97)

In Parāśara smṛti (2. 14-15), it is said that if śūdra-s abandon the prescribed service of three varṇa-s and do other things, their lifespan will be reduced.

विकर्मकुर्वते शूद्रा द्विजशुश्रूषयोज्झिताः 14

भवन्त्यल्पायुषस्ते वै निरयं यान्त्यसंशयं 15

'Abandoning the service to dvija, if a śūdra does other improper occupations, he will become short lived and undoubtedly go to hell (lower realm).'

Whenever the śāstra mentions that breaking a rule will reduce the lifespan of the individual, we need to understand that they are referring to something that will impact the individual biologically. These rules are not made for social reasons but for biological ones, with the intention of protecting the one for whom the rule is meant.

Mixed varṇa

So far, what we have looked into are the cases of pure varṇa, meaning both parents are of the same varṇa, and the resulting child is also of that varṇa. So, what happens in the case of mixed varṇa, that is, when the varṇa of the parents are different from that of each other?

If a man of a (vibrationally) higher varṇa marries a woman of a (vibrationally) lower varṇa, an anulōma child is born. If a woman of a higher varṇa marries a man of a lower varṇa, a pratilōma child is born. The word anulōma indicates that which is aligned with the natural direction, and pratilōma means that which is opposite or reverse of the natural direction. So while the śāstra-s permitted marriage between men of a higher varṇa and women of a lower varṇa, the opposite was discouraged (Manu X.10.41).[60] The reason had to do with how pratilōma affects the progeny and, hence, the entire lineage that follows.

In the case of mixed marriages, the child is lower in vibration than that of the father's varṇa, and the rules applied for the child are that of the mother's varṇa. This is why in anulōma marriages, the child of a brāhmaṇa man and a śūdra woman is not eligible for upanayana, although the child of a brāhmaṇa from a kṣatriya or vaiśya woman, or a kṣatriya man from vaiśya woman is eligible for upanayana as seen in (Manu III.12 to 19), Yājñavalkya (1.55 & 57), Vasiṣṭha (14. 5), etc.

The śāstra-s have given names for each such combination arising out of mixed varṇa-s and stated that only six of these are eligible for upanayana. Accordingly, among the pure varṇa-s and anulōma, these six are entitled to the upanayana saṃskāra: 1. The pure brāhmaṇa 2. The pure kṣatriya 3. The pure vaiśya 4. The son of a brāhmaṇa man and kṣatriya wife 5. The son of a kṣatriya man and a vaiśya wife 6. The son of a brāhmaṇa and a vaiśya wife. All other anulōma, as well as those born by illicit intercourse (without legal marriage) and all pratilōma, are to be treated as śūdra so far as initiation with sacred thread is considered.[61] To this list, Yājñavalkya added another, according to which, anulōma descendants of kṣatriya and vaiśya on females of immediately lower varṇa than themselves, resulting in the

---

60 स्वजातिजानन्तरजाः षट् सुता द्विजधर्मिणः ।

शूद्राणां तु सधर्माणः सर्वेऽपध्वंसजाः स्मृताः ॥ ४१ ॥ Manu (X.10.41)

61 According to Medatithi and Kulluka (commentators of Manu)

jāti named rathakara; he has a right to sacrifice, give alms and the upanayana sacrament.

Even in the case of a child of mixed varṇa, the change in varṇa is said to happen in successive generations of a mixed lineage (and not by changing guṇa-karma alone) under the following conditions as mentioned in Manu (X.64-65), Yaj. (I.96), Gautama (IV.18-19), etc.

As per Manu X.10.64,

शूद्रायां ब्राह्मणाज् जातः श्रेयसा चेत् प्रजायते ।

अश्रेयान् श्रेयसीं जातिं गच्छत्या सप्तमाद् युगात् ॥ ६४ ॥

'If the child born from a śūdra woman to a brāhmaṇa man goes on being wedded to a superior person—the inferior attains the superior varṇa, within the seventh generation.'—(64)

Yaj. (I.96)

जात्युत्कर्षो युगे ज्ञेयः सप्तमे पञ्चमेऽपि वा ।

व्यत्यये कर्मणां साम्यं पूर्ववच्चाधरोत्तरम् ॥ ९६ ॥

'Varṇa becomes elevated during the fifth or the seventh generation; (the use of 'api' means even in the sixth generation, as per Mitākṣara). Similarly after five, (six) or seven generations one acquires that varṇa of which he has followed the occupations.'

Thus, in the case of mixed marriages where the father is of a brāhmaṇa varṇa and the mother is of a śūdra varṇa, it is said that it takes seven generations of their daughter marrying a brāhmaṇa (in each generation), for the seventh generation child to be of a pure varṇa of a brāhmaṇa. This rise in varṇa is called jātyutkarṣa. Similarly, it takes five or six generations for the progeny of a brāhmaṇa father and a kṣatriya or vaiśya mother, respectively.

This is also confirmed by Gautama in the below verse.

Gautama (4.22-24).—'In the seventh generation, men obtain a change of varṇa, being either raised to a higher one or degraded to a lower one. The venerable teacher declares that this happens in the fifth generation, and the same rule applies to those born from parents of different varṇa that are intermediate between two of the varṇa originally created by Brahmā.'

Interestingly, the same happens even by following occupations of another varṇa in successive generations, as stated by Yājñavalkya, which is a clear indication that there was a subtle understanding of how vibrations alter by karma (occupations) as well as by birth, the result of which will manifest in the next generations.

Only if we understand this in terms of frequencies of vibrations of mixed varṇa-s can we solve the riddle of why such an injunction is made in the śāstra-s. The numbers seven, six and five here are important because they are direct indicators that it takes seven, six or five generations for the vibration in that lineage to ascend one cakra's vibration in each generation, based on whether it is a brāhmaṇa man marrying a śūdra woman, or any other intermediate combination.

Can a Guru change a person's varṇa?

When I asked a learned Master the question of whether a person of a vibrationally lower varṇa can become a higher varṇa in the same birth by adopting the guṇa-karma of a higher varṇa, he said that it is possible by the grace of a Guru alone, and only if the Guru decides to alter one's karma in such a manner. And then, he narrated the following story, which is of great significance in understanding this aspect.

The story is from the Śrī Guru Caritra (Chapter 27), which is a revered spiritual text from the 15ᵗʰ century.[62] This book has

---

62 The original version of the Guru Charitra is in Marathi, compiled by Śrī Saraswati Gangadhar, a disciple of Śrī Dattatreya during His incarnation as Śrī Narasimha Saraswati. Translations from the original text are available in other languages, especially in Kannada and Telugu, by Saraswathi Prakashan, Belgaum. Most of the incidents narrated in the book occur in the regions of Karnataka and Maharashtra.

documented several incidents from the life of the great Guru Śrī Dattatreya and his two subsequent incarnations as Śrīpada Śrī Vallabha and Śrī Narasimha Saraswati. Guru Śrī Dattareya is said to be a combined avatar of Brahma, Viṣṇu and Śiva. In one of the stories, it is described how Gurunath, in order to teach a lesson to two arrogant brāhmaṇa pandits, calls a random stranger walking on the street and changes his varṇa to that of a brāhmaṇa by making him cross seven lines. The story, in short, goes thus:

> When first enquired by Gurunath, the stranger says that he belongs to the Matanga community (which is vibrationally lower than the śūdra varṇa). In the story, Gurunath gave his danda (staff) to one of his disciples and asked him to draw seven lines on the ground in front of the Matanga. He then asked the Matanga man to cross each line. With each line that he crossed, Gurunath made the Matanga man mention his varṇa. Each time Gurunath asked him, 'What varṇa do you belong to?'
>
> With the first line, the Matanga replied that he belonged to Kirat Vamsa (the hunter class) and said that his name was Van Rakha. After crossing the second line, the Matanga said that he was Ganga Putra (i.e., belonging to the fisherman's community). After crossing the third, fourth and fifth lines, respectively, the Matanga said that he was a śūdra, a vaiśya and a kṣatriya. After crossing the seventh line, the Matanga replied that he was now a Brāhmaṇa devoted to Vedic study and began reciting Vedic mantra-s as Brahmadeva himself! This was accomplished by the grace of the Guru, who gave sacred ash to be besmeared all over the body of the Matanga, now turned into a Brāhmaṇa.
>
> Gurunath performed this miracle to teach a lesson to two arrogant brāhmaṇa pandits who, encouraged by a Nawab King, were using the Veda-s publicly for personal aggrandisement, inviting people to contest with them and making a mockery of it. As a consequence, the brāhmaṇa

pandits were said to have been cursed by Vedamāta to face death and live as Brahma rākṣasa-s for twelve years, owing to their misuse of the Veda-s.

As for the Matanga, he prayed to Gurunath to let him remain a brāhmaṇa permanently. Gurunath, in response to this request, told the Matanga that due to certain saṃskāra-s (habitual patterns) of this birth, he would not be able to be a true brāhmaṇa, even though he could now utter the scriptures by the Guru's blessings. Gurunath assured him that he would attain the varṇa of a brāhmaṇa through his blessings, but in the next birth. However, the Matanga was not satisfied and kept persisting that Gurunath should let him remain a brāhmaṇa in this birth itself. At that time, the Matanga's wife and children happened to arrive at the scene. When she approached him, the Matanga started beating her and driving her away (displaying the saṃskāra-s of his present birth as Matanga). The weeping wife prayed to Gurunath that he give her back her Matanga husband. In response to this, Gurunath instructed someone to pour water on the Matanga, thereby removing the sacred ash smeared on him. With this, the Matanga returned to his original state, forgetting all that happened.

This story reiterates the rules of the śāstra that even if one follows the guṇa or performs the karma of a higher varṇa, he doesn't become of that varṇa in the same birth. And even though a Guru might be able to change one's varṇa, it might not be the right thing to ask for. Therefore, under all ordinary circumstances and in the absence of a Guru's intervention, it should be understood that even with modifications of guṇa, it takes another birth for the subtle vibrations to obtain a physical body which is suitable to the modified guṇa.

In case there is still some confusion about whether a person can change their physical body's vibration and perform the karma assigned to another varṇa, may the words of Śrī Kṛṣṇa give clarity. Let us remember verse 47 of Chapter 18 of the Bhagvad Gītā, in which Śrī Kṛṣṇa talks about how it is better to perform one's own dharma, even if imperfectly done than to attempt to do another's dharma, even though perfectly.

श्रेयान्स्वधर्मो विगुण: परधर्मात्स्वनुष्ठितात् |

स्वभावनियतं कर्म कुर्वन्नाप्नोति किल्बिषम् || 47||

This verse has to be remembered whenever there arises confusion about whether or not a person belonging to one varṇa can do the karma pertaining to another. The verse's last line says that by doing one's innate duty, a person does not incur 'kilbiṣam.' The word kilbiṣa is often translated to mean 'sin', but it also means disease or injury, and could be the more apt meaning when we understand the biological impact of performing karma that is not vibrationally suitable to one's body.

Know your varṇa

As individuals who navigate through various emotions and associated activities even in a single day, it is natural that we operate from different cakra-s and manifest the associated guṇa. But there is a dominant cakra for each individual, which we remain in during the resting phase when outside influence is minimal. It is the frequency of vibration that we most resonate with in a given birth and what we go home to. It is this 'home state' that gives each of us our varṇa, which manifests as our svabhāva and is expressed as our inherent guṇa.

Since varṇa is a biological quality that is inherent in every human, there are ways in which those who are not born in a Hindu family[63] can find out their varṇa. The simplest way is to make an

---

63 Those born in Hindu families would know their inherent varṇa in many ways such as through surnames, hereditary vocations of their ancestors, food and other preferences, etc.

honest self-assessment of one's predominant guṇa-s since childhood and compare it with what is given in the Bhagavad Gītā and Śrīmad Bhāgavatam as mentioned in this chapter.

Another way to know varṇa is by becoming subtle and thereby being able to see the aura. After all, seeing is believing. Those who are able to, can know it by just looking at the centre of one's palm, held at arm's distance against a well-lit white background. As you focus on the centre of your palm, you will see a light through your peripheral vision, surrounding your palm and fingers. As you become more subtle, you will be able to see colours in this light. The colours seen early in the morning after a good night's sleep, in one's natural state, in the absence of disease, are likely to be the colours of one's inherent varṇa. This exercise can be carried out for a few months and compared with one's natural tendencies to gain clarity about the dominant colours in one's aura. When we are able to reach the stage of perceiving the subtle aura, we will realise that the system of varṇa applies to all.[64]

By becoming mindful of our present tendencies, working on enhancing the positive qualities, practising restraint with respect to the undesirable qualities, and performing karma in accordance with our varṇa, we purify the vibrations of our aura. When the aura is vibrationally pure, the resulting colours, whichever they may be, will be seen as bright light (śucayo varṇa), similar to that of the devatā-s. Reaching that state is the purpose of each individual's birth.

---

64 It is advisable to only attempt to see one's own aura and not that of others, for reasons which are beyond the scope of this work to explain.

Chapter 4: Varṇa as Sound

"Even the student of occultism, who has not been able to develop the clairvoyant vision to such a high degree, is soon able to develop the sense of psychic perception whereby he is able to at least 'feel' the vibrations of the aura, though he may not see the colours, and thus be able to interpret the mental states which have caused them. The principle is of course the same, as the colours are but the outward appearance of the vibrations themselves, just as the ordinary colours on the physical plane are merely the outward manifestation of vibration of matter."

– Swami Panchadasi, 'The Human Aura'[65]

Not many of us are gifted with clairvoyant vision, enabling us to see the aura, but almost all of us do have a natural ability to perceive the vibrations of the aura. We do it on a regular basis without even realising it. It is indeed a matter to contemplate that we refer to people we get along with as being 'of the same frequency' as us, and when we do not like someone, we say 'that person is of a different frequency.' Not only do we use a very technical term like frequency[66]

---

65 The Human Aura: Astral Colours and Thought Forms, by Swami Panchadasi, originally published in 1912 by Yogi Publication Society, Chicago.

66 Technically, Frequency refers to the number of waves that pass a fixed point, per unit time (per second). High frequency means that a large number of waves pass a point per second, and low frequency means that a fewer number of waves pass a point per second. Waves of a shorter wavelength have a high frequency, and waves of a broader wavelength have a lower

we also use another technical term called vibration[67] in our day-to-day expressions. We often say that such and such place has 'good vibes' or 'bad vibes.' Those who are more sensitive will even be able to perceive the nature of these 'vibes' we receive from some people, be it aggressive, motherly, fearful, sexual, etc., and we express this in daily colloquial language.

A popular quote says, 'If you want to find the secrets of the universe, think in terms of energy, frequency and vibration.'

This quote could be easily thought of as what one of the ṛṣi-s of ancient Bhārat would have said, but instead, it is a quote from the famous Nikola Tesla, the Serbian-American inventor. Whenever Western scientists came close to discovering universal cosmic laws, their inventions and discoveries were confined to the closed doors of expensive labs, peer groups and research institutes, as gadgets that only a section of society could afford or served a specific purpose, and thus left out advanced science from the day-to-day lives of the common man. True genius should have meant that a scientist should be able to translate their advanced discoveries into usable and practical day-to-day aspects of the life of the common man, offering it as a seva for the welfare of humanity. *That* is what the ṛṣi-s of Bhārat did.

In this chapter, as we skim through the fundamentals of sound, we will realise how ṛṣi-s took the most advanced concepts of science and brought them into implementable forms of social life for the welfare of mankind. Such a practical application of advanced science is unique to the Hindu civilisation.

---

frequency. Frequency (ν) is directly proportional to Energy (E) as per the equation $E = h\nu$, where h is Planck's constant. This means, when Frequency increases, Energy also increases and vice versa.

67 Technically, vibration means the back and forth oscillation of particles about their mean position. 'Frequency of vibration' is a term used to indicate the number of vibrations per second, and is measured in hertz (Hz).

Sound

The ṣaṭ-cakra-nirūpaṇa text shows the cakra-s represented as lotuses, with each petal of each lotus having specific alphabets of the saṃskṛtam language, indicating that sounds of the saṃskṛtam language are connected to specific cakra-s and therefore can create specific frequencies of vibration when uttered. The connection of sound to varṇa is also mentioned in ancient tantra texts such as the Śāradātilaka.

In the Śāradātilaka (I.56-57), Devī is described as śabdabrahmarūpiṇī. Śabdabrahma means unmanifest sound, and it is said to exist in human beings as the kuṇḍalinī and then appears as letters in prose, poetry, etc., being carried by vāyu (air) to the throat, palate, cerebral region, teeth, etc. producing specific sounds (क वर्ग, च वर्ग, ट वर्ग, त वर्ग, etc.). The sounds thus produced are called akṣara-s, and when written, they are spoken of as varṇa-s, that is, letters of the alphabet, mātṛkā, which are 50 from *a* (अ) to *kṣa* (क्ष).[68] In several Bhāratiya languages, the word used to refer to the series of alphabets is varṇamālā. This is what we shall now explore – Devī as 'mātṛka varṇa rūpiṇī' — the personification of alphabets, and therefore of sound.

Properties of sound

What did the ṛṣi-s know that made it possible to understand the finer nuances of sound? Did they know as much as we think we know today? Let us find out by exploring the properties of sound, both as defined by modern science and what the ṛṣi-s knew. Once we get an idea of the properties of sound as known to the ancient masters, we will explore how they used this knowledge to design the system of human classification based on varṇa as inherent sound capability.

---

68 Vide 'History of Dharmaśāstra' by Dr. Kane, Vol V, Part II, Sec VI, Ch. XXVI, Page 1099.

Wave series

As per modern science, sound propagates by disturbing the particles in the medium in which it travels. When an object vibrates, it creates pressure variation in the nearby particles of the medium. These areas of high pressure (compressions) and low pressure (rarefactions) constitute a complete sound wave. This is how modern science describes the propagation of sound waves in the air or any other medium, as depicted in the below image.

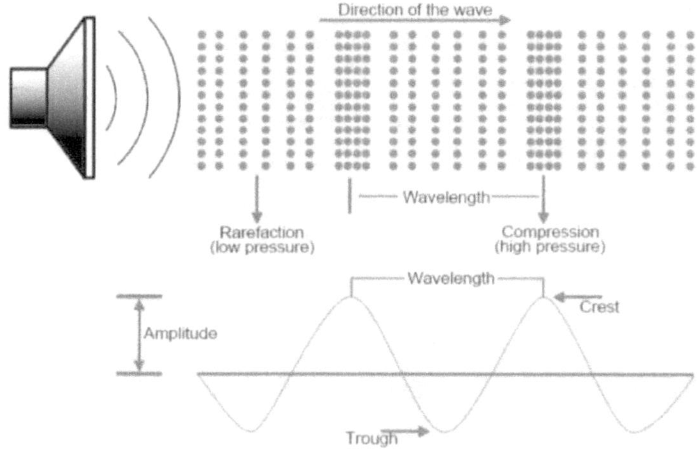

Ṛṣi Kaṇāda, the author of the 'Vaiśeṣika Sūtra', stated that sound is said to possess the attribute of being speedily destroyed[69] and is said to be produced from saṃyogāt (conjunction), vibhāgāt (disjunction) and an (existing) sound.[70] This description was used to explain the production of sound on the principle of ripples and waves. According to ancient scholars,[71] the first sound is produced from impact - for example, a drum and a drum stick - that is, through saṃyogā, within

---

69 गुणस्य सतोऽपवर्गः कर्म्मभिः साधर्म्यम् ॥ २ । २ । २५ - Vaiśeṣika Sūtra (2.2.25)

70 संयोगाद्विभागाच्च शब्दाच्च शब्दनिष्पत्तिः ॥ २ । २ । ३१ - Vaiśeṣika Sūtra (2.2.31)

71 Keshava Misra in Tarka Bhasha explains the vichī taraṅga nyāya based on the Vaiśeṣika Sūtra

the limits of that particular space. Then, outside that circle, the second sound is produced from the first and extends it. Then, the third sound is produced from the second, the fourth from the third and so on. This is the theory of successive production of a single sound. This is called the vicītaraṅga nyāya. The words 'vicītaraṅga' means 'wave', and 'nyāya' means law or phenomenon. By this phenomenon, it is proposed that sound originating from one point does not travel to the listener's ear directly but through a series of origination and destruction in what seems like waves. Thus, the ancient theory of vicītaraṅga nyāya proposed one of the earliest wave theories of sound.

Speed of sound

The speed of sound determines its vibrational ability. The faster the sound travels, the greater the disturbance of particles in the medium in which it travels, causing higher vibrations with increased speed. The speed of sound is influenced by the density of the medium through which it travels. The greater the density of a medium, the faster the speed of sound, as shown in the table below.[72]

Material	Density (g/cm)	Speed (m/s)
Air	0.00139	331.45
Helium	0.000178	965
Fat	0.95	1450
Water	1.00	1496
Muscle	1.07	1580
Skull Bone	1.91	4080
Steel	7.86	5940
Aluminium	2.58	6420
Copper	8.90	6420

Long before modern scientists learnt that sound changes its speed based on the density of the medium, with the speed of sound in air

---

72 Source: Multiple published studies on speed of sound in body tissue, in air, metals, etc.

(331 m/s) being less than that in water (1496 m/s) which is lesser than that within the body (muscles 1580 m/s) and much higher in the skull bone (4080 m/s), ṛṣi-s classified japa (mantra chanting) based on this property as vācika (audibly uttered), upāṃśu (inaudibly uttered) and mānasa (mentally revolved), with each succeeding one being superior to each proceeding one.[73]

The understanding of the ṛṣi-s came through the experience that when we listen to sounds externally, the medium of air which carries the sound waves to our ear reduces the vibration in the process. Whereas when we ourselves utter the chant, the sound travels down the vocal tube. This is because the length of the vocal tube from the lips to the glottis is smaller than the wavelength of sound, so the vocal tube carries the sound downwards. As the sound travels downward inside the body, its speed increases due to the density of blood, flesh and bones. When the speed of sound increases, its vibration also increases. Further, when japa is done only by mental thought or mental repetition (by those who have memorised it), it will have the highest vibration owing to its increased speed due to the impact of the thought vibration on the skull, which has a high density. This is why women and the śūdra varṇa are instructed to only listen to chants and sacred texts recited by others and not to read, chant (or memorise) them themselves.

---

73 Narasimha Purāṇa (Chapter 58, verses 78 – 81) given below

जपयज्ञं ततः कुर्यात् गायत्रीं वेदमातरम्। त्रिविधो जपयज्ञं स्यात्तस्य भेदं निबोधत ॥ ७८ ॥ वाचिकश्च उपांशुश्च मानसस्त्रिविधः स्मृतः । त्रयाणां जपयज्ञानां श्रेयः स्यादुत्तरोत्तरम् ॥ ७९ ॥ यदुच्चनीचस्वरितैः स्पष्टशब्दवदक्षरैः । शब्दमुच्चारयेद्वाचा जपयज्ञः स वाचिकः ॥ ८० ॥

'Japa is of three kinds. i.e. Vācika, Upāṃśu and Mānasa. Out of these japa-s, upāṃśu is better than vācika and mānasa japa is the best. When the person engaged in japa pronounces the words with a clear echo of every letter in low, high and equal tone, it is called the vācika japa. When the hymns are pronounced slowly by moving the lips up and down slightly and the person engaged in it listens to or understands the hymn, this japa is called upāṃśu. When every letter, pada and word meaning of the group of hymns is absorbed by mental concentration, it is called mānasa japa.'

Temperature impacts sound

Modern science understands that increases in temperature cause sound to travel at a greater speed. Sound is transmitted through the air by compression waves, which, at a small scale, depend on molecules transferring energy from one to another. Air molecules have more energy at higher temperatures, which means they vibrate faster. This allows the sound waves to travel faster because they are propelled by collisions between the molecules. Kimberly Strong, a professor of physics at the University of Toronto, says, 'The speed of sound changes by about 0.6 metres per second for every degree (increase in temperature).'[74]

All the Vedic fire rituals which involve chanting mantra-s to the sacred agni are based on this principle. The sound that travels faster through hot air causes the vibrations to increase and carry it to those who are participating in the fire ritual. Mantra-s chanted to the fire have greater speed and consequently higher vibratory capacity.

Sound patterns

In the 1960s and 70s, the detailed experiments of Dr. Hans Jenny on Cymatic phenomena gained popularity and are documented in a book and film titled Cymatics. He proved through experiments that different sounds would produce different patterns. Low-frequency sounds produced simple geometric shapes. As the sound frequency was increased, these simple forms would break up, and more complex patterns would appear. Many of the patterns created by the sound resembled the cell structures of plants and animals. Some of the geometric patterns resembled the mandala-s used in Eastern spiritual traditions. Dr. Jenny came to the conclusion that each individual cell generates its own sound, and groups of cells also generate their own sounds, as do the organs of the body. He found that these sounds are harmonically related to each other. Indeed, the entire human body

---

74 CBC Radio Article: 'Does the speed of sound change with temperature?' Posted: February 01, 2019

has its own sound made up of all the sounds of its cells, tissues and organs.[75]

Dr. Hans Jenny, with his cymatic study equipment, and the mandala-like patterns formed at different frequencies. Source: https://www.delamora.life/cymatics

It is likely that when the ṛṣi-s of Bhārat declared that Śabdabrahma is the source of creation, they were referring to a much finer and detailed understanding of what Dr. Jenny called Cymatics. The ṛṣi-s described sound at four subtle levels of manifestation: parā, paśyantī, madhyama and vaikharī. The tantra texts describe the impulse to sound production arising in the mūlādhāra cakra as parā (vāk); it is called paśyantī when it reaches the svādhiṣṭhāna cakra, madhyama in the heart, and vaikharī in the mouth. All the mantra-s that are uttered in vaikharī form are evolved from the varṇa-s of the alphabets that are deemed to be living conscious sound powers. The bīja mantra-s (such as hrīm, srīm, etc.) are said to make the form of the devatā manifest. This means every devatā śakti is the manifested form of a sound of a particular frequency, which we call the mantra of that devatā. By tuning into that frequency (through the mantra), we connect with that particular devatā-śakti.

---

75 Dr. Jenny, Hans. Cymatics: A Study of Wave Phenomena and Vibration Vol I (1967) and Vol II (1974)

The unique shapes and forms of some Hindu deities are perhaps these sound frequencies seen and experienced by ṛṣi-s in deep meditative states when they connected to specific frequencies.

Rhythm in biology

A 2014 study titled 'Life Rhythm as a Symphony of Oscillatory Patterns'[76] describes how 'rhythms can communicate bio-information that governs a wide variety of functions, including that of guiding living beings towards health and well-being.' The study provided evidence that 'from the cellular level to the whole organism, every signalling event is fashioned by rhythms as vibratory patterns.' The study showed that changes in the rhythms and modes of interaction of subcellular oscillators can result in remarkable modulation of gene expression and cellular dynamics, playing an essential role in states of wellness and disease.

More recent studies indicate that the DNA nucleotide has musical rhythms. In some studies,[77,78] the researchers sought to generate rhythms out of DNA and even compose a musical piece out of a gene's rhythmic sequence. There are also sonification studies that primarily generate melodies out of a gene sequence.[79]

Ages before modern science began understanding the impact of rhythmic sound on human biology, the ṛṣi-s of Bhārat spoke of chandas and classified all poetic compositions and mantra-s based

---

76　Muehsam D, Ventura C. Life rhythm as a symphony of oscillatory patterns: electromagnetic energy and sound vibration modulates gene expression for biological signaling and healing. Glob Adv Health Med. 2014 Mar;3(2):40-55. doi: 10.7453/gahmj.2014.008. PMID: 24808981; PMCID: PMC4010966.

77　Yanez, Alvaro. The Musical Geometry of Genes. Generating Rhythms from DNA. Leonardo Music Journal, Vol. 29, pp. 45–49, 2019

78　Fesenmeier, Samuel. Coding DNA into Music: An Alternate Way of Analysis. Honors Thesis. University of Dayton, 2015.

79　J. Dunn and M.A. Clark. Life Music: The Sonification of Proteins. Leonardo 32, No. 1, 23–32 (1999).

on chandas. The ṛṣi-s understood that each type of chandas produces a different rhythmic pattern. They took this understanding a level deeper when they stated that individuals, too, fundamentally operate with a particular chandas, the upkeeping of which creates health and well-being in the individual.

It is this understanding with which they referred to the brāhmaṇa as being born with the gāyatrī chandas, kṣatriya the triṣṭubh chandas and vaiśya as the jagatī chandas. The śūdra, on the other hand, was said to not possess an inherent chandas, meaning that the śūdra has a naturally discordant system. The understanding of the ṛṣi-s was so fine that even the popular Savitṛ mantra (which we call the Gāyatrī mantra) was to be recited differently by each of the three varṇa-s, as per some of the gṛhya-sutra texts.[80] The name Gāyatrī itself is the name of the chandas, not of the mantra. This is an indication that the ṛṣi-s recognised an inherently different rhythmic pattern in each varṇa, and prescribed mantra-s that would bring the individual's body in alignment with their inherent rhythm.

But why were the ṛṣi-s so particular about one varṇa not uttering the mantra-s meant for another, especially a vibrationally higher varṇa? To find the answer, we must understand the concept of resonant frequency and what happens when an individual goes beyond their body's resonant frequency.

---

80 As per Sankhayana Gṛhya Sūtra II.5, 4 to 6, the triṣṭubh which is to be taught as the Savitri to Kṣatriya students is: ā kṛṣṇena rajasā (Rg. I.35.2) and the Jagati Savitri for the vaiśya is: hiraṇyāpāṇiḥ savitā (Rg. I.35.9) or haṃsaḥ śuciṣad (Rg IV.40.5). Vide Dr. P.V. Kane's History of Dharmaśāstra.' Vol I, Part 2. These mantra-s from the ṚgVeda are given below:

(Rg. I.35.2) for Kṣatriya varna

आ कृष्णेन रजसा वर्तमानो निवेशयन्नमृतं मर्त्यं च ।

हिरण्ययेन सविता रथेना देवो याति भुवनानि पश्यन् ॥

(Rg. I.35.9) for Vaiśya Varna

हिरण्यपाणिः सविता विचर्षणिरुभे द्यावापृथिवी अन्तरीयते ।

अपामीवां बाधते वेति सूर्यमभि कृष्णेन रजसा द्यामृणोति ॥

Resonant frequency

Resonant frequency is the natural frequency where a medium vibrates at the highest amplitude. Resonance is an important factor when examining sound and its quality because when the frequency of forced vibrations on a body matches the body's natural frequency, a dramatic increase in amplitude occurs. This means that our organs and systems have their own innate or resonant frequencies. Anything less than the resonant frequency will not cause harm, whereas anything more than the resonant frequency can throw the body into stress mode, with the individual experiencing loss of energy (prāṇa) and eventually manifesting disease.

At the gross physical level, many studies have been undertaken to evaluate the human body's resonant frequency to assess the body's impact upon exposure to whole-body vibration. At the resonant frequency, there is maximum displacement between the organ and the skeletal structure, placing biodynamic strain on the body tissue involved. This understanding is used to design industrial buildings and transport systems so that the exposure to vibration close to the body's resonant frequency may be minimised.[81] In these studies, the range of resonant frequency of the participants was found to be between 5 Hz to 10 Hz based on the seated/standing/reclining posture and the vibration magnitude to which the participants were exposed. In these studies, the focus was on the externally experienced mechanically generated vibration. These values are different from those which would be generated through internal vibration using sound. We see this in the following example.

Using the modern understanding of entrainment whereby one rhythmic vibrating object will synchronise with the other, a study[82]

---

81 James M. W. Brownjohn, Xiahua Zheng. Discussion of human resonant frequency. Second International Conference on Experimental Mechanics, Fook Siong Chau, Chenggen Quan, Editors, Proceedings of SPIE Vol. 4317 (2001)

82 Acoustical Resonance in Humans through Determination of Individual Natural Frequency (Physics) by Anirvan Gupta, Nivedita Azad. International Journal of Science and Research (IJSR), ISSN: 2319-7064 (2018)

was conducted with 30 subjects, 15 males and 15 females from various age groups of 15 years to 55 years, and they were exposed to sound notes of frequencies in the human audible range (20 Hz to 20,000 Hz). The particular frequency at which an individual experiences maximum vibrations from within was noted. This frequency was then related to the resonant frequency of the human body's inner cavity. The study found that the resonant frequency for each individual was different.

The understanding that every individual has a different resonant frequency is important to contemplate. This means that each individual is healthiest when they operate at the frequency that resonates with their own.

The ṛṣi-s of ancient Bhārat seemed to know the resonant frequency of individuals as being different and classified them into broader categories of varṇa, and then they prescribed specific mantra-s for each varṇa, and insisted that the mantra-s meant for one was not for the other. Wherever the same mantra was prescribed for all, it is likely that it was a lower frequency mantra which would suit the person with the lowest resonant frequency (this is likely to be the case with the modern version of the Savitṛ/Gāyatrī mantra, which has been modified by adding the vyāhṛti-s bhūr, bhuvah and svāhā)[83] so that even misuse of the mantra (meaning, it is used by those for whom it was not originally meant) will cause lesser damage.

Interestingly, a study[84] looked at the innate 'resting' or resonant frequencies of different parts of the body and has come up with data resembling the points in the figure below.

We see in this figure that the measure of frequency of vibration increases as we go from external parts of the body to internal parts

---

83 Joseph, Sinu. 'Rtu Vidya: Ancient Science Behind Menstrual Practices', Chapter 10 – Mantras and their effect on menstrual cycles, 2020.

84 Hasa, R & Liedl, T & Bucha, Jozef. (2018). The comfort of the passengers. IOP Conference Series: Materials Science and Engineering. 294. 012015. 10.1088/1757-899X/294/1/012015.

and organs. Thus, we see that the frequency of vibration of the external parts, such as the legs, is shown as being between 2 Hz to 20 Hz based on the posture, that of the arms as 5 Hz to 10 Hz, and that of the head as 20 Hz to 30 Hz. The frequency of the internal parts, such as the abdominal mass, is 4 Hz to 8 Hz, the spinal column is 10 Hz to 12 Hz, the chest wall is 50 Hz to 100 Hz, and interocular structures are 20 Hz to 90 Hz. Had they gone further to the level of cells, the frequencies would perhaps have further increased.

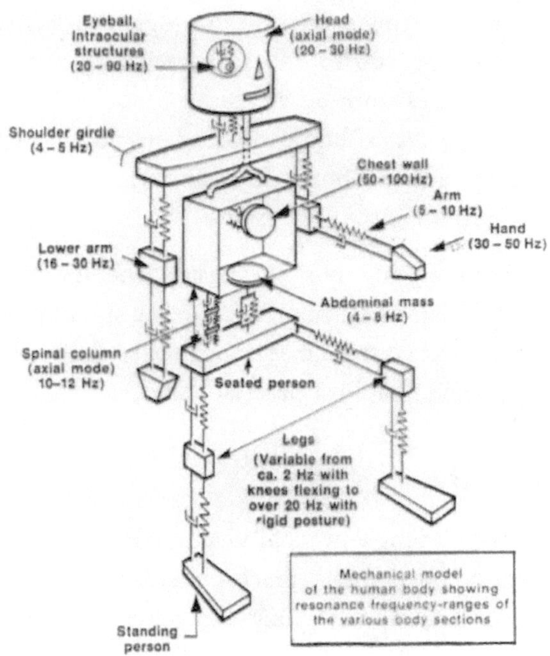

This modern mechanical representation should bring to mind the ancient Puruṣa Sūkta describing the different varṇa-s as originating from different parts of the body of the divine Puruṣa. It is hard to miss the correlation that each varṇa was a reference to the lowest to highest frequency of vibration, starting from the feet (śūdra) to the mouth/head (brāhmaṇa).

Vibratory Medicine

Over the last seventy-five years or so, modern science has come to acknowledge a system of medicine called 'Vibratory Medicine', under which comes the popular name of 'Vibroacoustic Therapy' (VAT), which uses low-frequency sound therapy (similar to music therapy), and Whole Body Vibration (WBV) which uses mechanical vibration for therapy, especially in sports. WBV typically uses frequencies below 30 Hz, while VAT uses 30 Hz to 120 Hz.

A look at the published study 'Possible Mechanisms for the Effects of Sound Vibration on Human Health'[85] gives us an overview of the number of existing studies on this topic, where the focus is on low-frequency sound (up to 250 Hz), including infrasound (1–16 Hz). All these studies work on creating vibrations for therapy at the level of the gross physical body, focusing on blood (hemodynamic), brain (neurological) and bone (musculoskeletal) by administering vibrations at the level of the ear or skin.

The methods of using sound or music as therapy in the West have involved several trials and errors, and they are still not quite sure how it works. Quite different from that is the precise ability of healing with music therapy using Bhāratiya classical music.

Music for Therapy

In her book 'The Healing Power of Indian Ragas', Smt. Rajam Shanker[86] has explained the phenomenal precision with which Bhāratiya rāga-s can be used for therapy pertaining to a wide range of physical and

85 Bartel L, Mosabbir A. Possible Mechanisms for the Effects of Sound Vibration on Human Health. Healthcare (Basel). 2021 May 18;9(5):597. doi: 10.3390/healthcare9050597. PMID: 34069792; PMCID: PMC8157227.

86 'The Healing Power of Ragas.' Rajam Shanker. Personal experiences of Ragas applied in music therapy. 2019. Smt. Rajam is a Life Member of NADA Centre for Music Therapy & Research India, a member of Indian Music Therapy Association (IMTA), has been a member of the World Federation of Music Therapy (WMTA) and International Association for

mental health issues. Smt. Shanker has over four decades of experience with Carnatic classical music and was initiated by her Guru into the practice of 'Indian Traditional Music Therapy.' In her book, along with several experiences of healing people through music, she has shared how exactly it works. Smt. Shanker has described from the ancient text Saṃgītaratnākara the description of the seven cakra-s corresponding to the seven svara-s.[87] Composed by Śārṅgadeva during the 13th century, both Carnatic music and Hindustani music traditions of Bhāratiya classical music regard Saṃgītaratnākara as a definitive text.

The description of cakra-s in Saṃgītaratnākara is very detailed and includes the location of the cakra, the number of petals, and, interestingly, the emotion or quality associated with each petal of the cakra. It also mentions the start point of numbering the petals, and a name is assigned to each petal so that the emotions/qualities can be assigned to the appropriate petals. This is important because, in Bhāratiya classical music, every rāga (melody) touches upon specific petals of different cakra-s based on the healing purpose it is meant to serve. To understand this better, as an example, let us take a look at the mūlādhāra cakra description as per Saṃgītaratnākara, mentioned in Smt. Shanker's book.

Figure: Muladhara Chakra
(Source: Wikipedia)

The verses describing Mūlādhāra cakra are as follows:

गुदलिङ्गान्तरे चक्रमाधाराख्यं चतुर्दलम् ।

परमः सहजस्तद्वदानन्दो वीरपूर्वकः ॥ १२० ॥

योगानन्दश्च तत्र स्यादैशानादिदले फलम् ।

अस्ति कुण्डलिनी ब्रह्मशक्तिराधारपङ्कजे ॥ १२१ ॥

Music & Medicine (IAMM). She has been conferred with the title 'Bharatiya Nadachikitsa Seva Chetana' and several other awards and recognitions.

87 There are essentially seven swaras in Carnatic music called Sa, Ri, Ga, Ma, Pa, Dha, Ni which is synonymous to C, D, E, F, G, A, B in the Western music.

The first line describes the cakra as located between the anus and reproductive organ and having four petals. The quality associated with each petal, starting from the petal in the East, is:

1. Brahmam petal of Mūlādhāra cakra is active when one is in a meditative state, unaware of sun, rain or other external stimuli

2. Sahajam petal is normally active for everyone

3. The Veeranandam petal gets activated when you accomplish a seemingly impossible feat, during the joy you feel when overcoming obstacles

4. The petal of Yuganandam is activated during yoga nidram, when communion is achieved by doing asana-s, and when kuṇḍalinī is awakened.

When a particular rāga touches a specific petal, there is a rush of prāṇa to that petal, making its quality dominant. The text also mentions those petals which are not to be touched for music, as it would be detrimental to music. For example, in the description of the Anāhata (heart) cakra, which has 12 petals, it is mentioned in Smt. Shanker's book:

> "The petals of the heart cakra are related to the ātma or soul. The life force in the petals of Asaidhal (movement), Virumbhudal (desire), Vivekam (discernment) and Ahankaram (Ego) are able to understand music. The other petals of the heart cakra are detrimental to music."

Similarly, in the case of Viśuddhi cakra having sixteen petals, the petals numbered eight to fifteen correspond to the seven svarā-s and a person in whom these are active is said to be blessed with musical ability. However, if the sixteenth petal is activated, that is harmful to music.

This sort of precise qualitative understanding of music, its effect on the body and mind, and its application through rāga-s for healing is the product of the compassionate genius of the ṛṣi-s of Bhārat.

Difference between music and mantra

Classical Bhāratiya music is based on the precise knowledge of cakra-s and designed to target specific problem areas that help to repair, rejuvenate or simply enhance well-being. Unlike the mantra, classical Bhāratiya music has no strict restrictions, even though such music works on the subtle level of cakra-s, just as mantra-s do. So then, what is the difference between classical music and mantra?

While classical Bhāratiya music is designed to have a healing purpose primarily for physical and mental well-being, mantra-s, especially from the Vedic era, are designed for spiritual fulfilment. Yes, there are some mantra-s such as those in Atharva Veda or Tantra, that have a healing or medicinal purpose, but these are to be administered by the healer who is a Guru or has been initiated for this purpose by a Guru and are not for self-recitation by ordinary people.

So the thing that separates music and mantra in its application is perhaps this - the petals that the rāga-s do not touch in music are touched by mantra-s while chanting.

For example, some of the excluded petals in rāga-s induce neutrality in thinking and a sense of detachment from worldly affairs, which would be needed in the spiritual path but could be a hurdle for those engaged in saṃsāra (worldly pursuits). Another example is that of the 16th petal of the Viśuddhi cakra, which is called Viś (poison) — activating this is necessary for spiritual progress as Viśuddhi is the mokṣa dvār and one needs to go through this to go to the next level of the Ājña cakra. However, this Viś petal could bring out a lot of poison, not just of the physical body but also of the karmic cycle pertaining to many births. This could manifest as a physical ailment, mental issues and major shifts in one's karmic cycle. This would be too much for an ordinary, uninitiated person to handle, and hence, this 16th petal of the Viśuddhi is not touched in music meant for an ordinary person.

Moreover, some of the mantra-s, such as the bīja mantra-s of each cakra, activate the entire cakra by invoking the śakti in that region. This is only needed in case of the spiritual path where it is necessary to activate the kuṇḍalinī śakti and cause it to surge upwards, piercing through each of the cakra-s. Even a layperson should know that experimenting with kuṇḍalinī is like playing with fire and must never be done without appropriate guidance from an experienced Guru.

Dangers of cakra activation for the uninitiated

Although this section might seem like a deviation from the main topic, given the rising popularity of cakra meditation, cakra cleansing, cakra activation, etc., using mantra-s, it is necessary to explain why this is not recommended unless strict prior preparation is done. Even though the frequencies of women (of menstrual age) and the śūdra varṇa corresponds to that of the lower cakra-s, for them too, mantra-s aimed at cakra activation/opening, even if it is only of the lower cakra is not recommended, without appropriate preparation. Let us understand why this is so.

When a cakra is activated through bīja mantra-s or other mantra-s, it will cause the sudden movement of prāṇa in that region. If one has problems associated with a specific cakra, the prāṇa in that cakra might have a diseased and stagnant quality to it, with accumulated subtle toxins (called āmā). In such cases, the mantra could cause sudden movement of the blocked or stagnant prāṇa and toxins. This might even give an immediate feeling of relief, but that will only be temporary. When healing is correctly performed, the diseased prāṇa and accumulated toxins will be flushed out of the system through the connecting channels. The subtle channels that carry prāṇa are called nāḍi. Unless a person is overall healthy, meaning the nāḍi-s are also clear, the stagnant prāṇa and āmā which are pushed out of the cakra will simply get stuck in the nāḍi. This accumulation of toxins in the nāḍi will start to affect the organs in that region, causing a different sort of disease. So, the person might feel that they have got some relief from one problem, but soon there will be another because the toxins have not been flushed out properly. This is why the primary preparation for any sort of direct work on cakra-s has to include the following:

1. Deha śuddhi: purification of the physical body through the right diet and yogāsana. A number of strict rules have to be followed in the type and quantity of food consumed for such practices. Further, before working on cakra-s, the practitioner should have the ability to hold any one āsana for at least three hours at a stretch. Only then will the body be steady enough for the mind to attain the needed focus.

2. Nādi śuddhi: purification of the nādi-s through long-term practice of specific types of prāṇāyāma meant for kuṇḍalinī yoga, under the guidance of an experienced Guru

3. Manas śuddhi: purification of the mind by cultivating positive thoughts, healthy habits and practice of self-restraint while engaging the senses. This is the section of yama and niyama that Patanjali-s Yoga Sūtra lists as the first two steps before undertaking any form of kriya yoga practice.

A cakra can be compared to a traffic junction and the connecting nādi-s to intersecting roads. If we turn the signal green, the traffic will certainly move out of the junction, but if the road ahead is blocked, the traffic will simply pile up on the road. The same is the case with mantra-s used for direct cakra activation without preparing the body.

If one is keen to use sound for physical well-being, then classical Bhāratiya music is a much safer method to work on the cakra-s, with the help of a classical music therapist, rather than experimenting with mantra-s without initiation and guidance from a Guru. Further, if one is intent upon cleansing cakra-s, the safest method would be to purify the qualities/emotions associated with each cakra by changing one's behaviour and thoughts.

Repercussions

So far, we have understood that each individual has a resonant frequency, which is the vibrational upper limit of each person's physical body. Exceeding this limit can cause the body to go into stress mode, eventually manifesting as a disease. At the atomic level, when the exposed frequency exceeds the resonant frequency, a large number of electrons in the atoms jump out of their orbits in search of the higher energy orbit. But if the body's natural capacity is of a lower frequency/energy, the loosened electrons cause the atoms to turn into free radicals, causing the body to go into oxidative stress. Oxidative stress, when unchecked, manifests in the form of various issues ranging from ageing to DNA mutation to even cancer.

For women of menstrual age, when the body receives high vibration beyond its capacity to handle, the resulting oxidative stress induces menstruation (before time) because the body's natural mechanisms recognise sudden oxidative stress as the time of menstruation.[88] In the language of prāṇa and apāna, the sudden upward rise of prāṇa in high vibrational places induces a forced balance in women's bodies by triggering the downward moving apāna to prevent the body from damage. This is the reason why women of menstrual age unexpectedly begin menstruating, or their cycles become irregular after visiting certain temples, as mentioned in chapter one.

In the body of a male, oxidative stress might be experienced as a feeling of causeless tiredness or exhaustion initially, which could later trigger the onset of different diseases. If this happens for those who are into spiritual practices or rituals, it is an indication that they are being exposed to high frequencies which are beyond their body's resonant frequency. This could happen for a person of a kṣatriya varṇa who is exposed to vibrations of a brāhmaṇa varṇa; for

---

88 Refer 'Ṛtu Vidyā: Ancient Science behind Menstrual Practices' for details on oxidative stress during menstruation.

a vaiśya varṇa individual who is exposed to vibrations of a kṣatriya or brāhmaṇa varṇa, and certainly for the śūdra varṇa and women of menstrual age who are exposed to vibrations of any of the other three varṇa-s.

With this understanding, we need to contemplate the rules for officiating as arcaka-s and conducting pūjā in temples, as given in chapter two. The Devapratiṣṭhātattva's rule as to who can perform prāṇa pratiṣṭhā for whom seems to be clear evidence of the above understanding. A brāhmaṇa can perform the prāṇa pratiṣṭhā for Viṣṇu, while a kṣatriya can do it for a vaiśya or śūdra yajamāna, and a vaiśya can do it for a śūdra yajamāna. The śūdra varṇa, having the lowest frequency of vibration, will struggle to invoke deities as needed for prāṇa pratiṣṭhā. Any slip in the process can create serious energy imbalances for the performing individual as well as the community around the temple.

An analogy to understand this better is how we select electrical appliances. When considering the capacity of the power supply, a general thumb rule is that it is better to have more power than we need because we should not run the power supply at 100% capacity. For example, it is better to have a 250-watt power supply and use it to run an appliance that requires 100 watts rather than having a 100-watt power supply and running it to full capacity. Essentially, the power supply should not overpower the appliance.

While the rule is very strict as to who can do the prāṇa pratiṣṭhā and invoke the deity in a temple, there seems to be some allowances made when it comes to daily pūjā. In the case of those temples where the deity is meant for the śūdra varṇa or for women of menstrual age, a person of the śūdra varṇa or women (when they are not menstruating) can also officiate as the arcaka, by following the specific rules for the given temple. For example, temples for resolving fertility issues or temples having the fierce forms of devatā-s.

However, a word of caution must be sounded as to why it is still dangerous and a slippery slope for women and the śūdra varṇa to act as arcaka-s. This is explained in the following section.

Sahasrāra, Pineal and DMT

The rules in the dharmaśāstra texts are extremely strict about not letting a person of the śūdra varṇa even listen to the Veda-s being chanted. There is punishment prescribed for the one who chants it in the presence of a śūdra, as well as for the śūdra who intentionally listens to it, knowing that he should not (Gautama XII.4). In the Rāmāyan too, there is the episode of Śrī Ram killing Shambuka, a śūdra, for studying the Veda-s. This is one of the most difficult-to-explain episodes of the Rāmāyan, causing some to even say that this was a manipulated version and not what Valmiki would have written. Śrī Ram's birth and life were only meant to upkeep dharma; everything he did was towards that goal, including the killing of Shambuka. So now let us understand the reason for this.

The chanting of the Veda-s and performance of the rituals by brāhmaṇa-s, the practice of hatha yoga, kuṇḍalinī yoga and the process of prāṇa pratiṣṭhā - these cause the opening of the sahasrāra cakra located in the crown of the head, in those who are sensitive enough. Just as the pituitary gland is triggered by activation of the ājña cakra (between the eyebrows), the pineal gland is triggered by activation of the sahasrāra cakra. The pineal is deep-seated inside the brain in a way that seems to be a conscious design of nature to protect it and prevent it from being casually triggered through external means. What is the role of the pineal, and why is it so protected?

Only when the sahasrāra cakra is activated is the pineal activated, and only then can a human communicate with other dimensions. The ritual offerings to pitṛ-s or devatā-s yield results only when performed by one in whom the sahasrāra can be opened and contact established with the devatā-s and pitṛ-s. While the sahasrāra can be triggered and activated by anyone who performs the sādhanā for it, why did the śāstra-s largely encourage only the brāhmaṇa man to preside over such rituals?

The highest vibrational frequency is only possible through the body of a brāhmaṇa man; therefore, through him alone can we access the higher vibrational realms of specific devatā-s and pitṛ-s. When those of other lower vibrational capacities try to access other dimensions, they will only reach that dimension, the frequency of which matches their own, obviously. In the case of the śūdra varṇa or menstruating women, if they opened the sahasrāra, they will connect to low-frequency realms similar to their own vibrational frequency. If the person has a dominant negative emotion such as kāma (lust), krodha (anger), lobha (greed), etc., they will attract beings which have similar qualities through resonance, since each emotion attracts a particular frequency of vibration that matches the emotion. Some of these realms can be dangerous to the individual as well as to society at large.

This understanding seems to be evidenced in the experiment carried out by Dr. Rick Strassman, M.D., who injected synthetic DMT into volunteers to study what happens when the pineal gland is triggered.[89] DMT (short for Dimethyltryptamine), a powerful, naturally occurring hallucinogenic compound, is a molecule present in some plants and in the animal kingdom. In the human body, scientists found that it is produced naturally by the pineal gland at the time of birth, death and during psychedelic experiences such as deep meditation (samādhi).

Dr. Strassman conducted DEA-approved clinical research at the University of New Mexico from 1990 to 1995 in which he injected sixty volunteers with synthetic DMT, and studied the effects. His detailed account of those sessions is documented in his book 'DMT: The Spirit Molecule.' Much to his own surprise, almost all the

---

89 Strassman M.D., Rick. DMT: The Spirit Molecule. Originally published in 2000.

volunteers injected with DMT had out-of-body experiences and made contact with 'alien' realms and strange beings, which was not always pleasant. Some saw ancient alphabets which they couldn't recognise; some were experimented upon by insect-like beings, and only a few experienced a divine soothing light. The experiences of the volunteers in the study seem to clearly indicate that DMT's effect as being pleasant or unpleasant had to do with the emotional state and related vibrational ability of the volunteers. Those who had animalistic tendencies by nature had frightening experiences with animal-like strange beings that were violent with them, and only a few who had a sattvic outlook contacted the divine higher realms and had pleasant experiences.

Towards the end of the study, Dr. Strassman himself underwent quite a few problems. One intuitive Mexican lady (his massage therapist), in fact, tells him that she could see evil spirits hovering around him, trying to access this plane through him and the study of this drug. In response to this message, Dr. Strassman writes: "Whether metaphorical, symbolic or real, there was a tremendous amount of negativity piling up around me. What to do? I didn't have to wait much longer for the solution, nor did I directly choose it. Rather, it came my way in a frightening manner." What happened next was that his wife suddenly developed cancer. At the same time, his stepson had become depressed and dropped out of school while living with his father in Canada. Upon his wife's request, he moved to Canada to be near family while she recuperated, thereby slowing down the pace of the study. Eventually, his marriage ended in a divorce.

Basically, it seemed like the study had opened up a channel whereby the beings from other realms were able to enter our dimension through those who took DMT, leading to unpleasant incidents. The happenings around the study should have sounded alarm bells to the doctor, but instead, he chose to ignore them with his rational intellect. This happened even though he received warnings from his spiritual advisers. For example, a Buddhist monastery that he was associated with and was on positive terms with, completely distanced themselves when he wrote in an article suggesting that monks could try DMT to experience enlightenment faster! In response, a letter from one of the female monks of the monastery read:

> "An attempt to induce enlightenment experiences by chemical means can never, will never, succeed. What it will do is badly confuse people and result in serious consequences for you."

Another letter from the head (Abbot) of the monastery read:

> "That DMT might elicit enlightenment experiences is delusional and contrary to the teachings of the Buddha; Hallucinogens disorder and confuse the mind, impede religious training, and can be a cause of rebirth into realms of confusion and suffering. This is the viewpoint of myself (the Abbot), the order and the whole of Buddhism. We urge you to cease all such experiments."

All of the above has been dutifully documented in his book.

The experience of the DMT-injected volunteers and the realms they contacted might help us understand why the śāstra-s refer to the śūdra as a burial ground.[90] It also explains why some of the rules given in chapter two say that women and the śūdra-s who chant the prohibited mantra-s (such as Gāyatrī, om, etc.) will go to adholoka (lower worlds) upon death.

---

90 In Vāsiṣṭa Dharmasūtra (17.11-12), it is written:

शव इति मृताख्या एके वा एतच्छमशानं ये शूद्राः ११ तस्माच्छूद्रसमीपे नाध्येतव्यम् १२ अथापि यमगीताञ्श्लोकानुदाहरन्ति श्मशानमेतत्प्रत्यक्षं ये शूद्राः पापचारिणः तस्माच्छूद्रसमीपे तु नाध्येतव्यं कदा चन १३

'Some call the śūdra race a burial-ground – 11 Therefore (the Veda) must not be recited in the presence of a śūdra – 12 Now they quote also the (following) verses, which Yama proclaimed: 'The śūdra-race is manifestly a burial-ground. Therefore (the Veda) must never be recited in the presence of a śūdra.' – 13

The Veda-s and mantra-s are not sterile poetry. They are consecrated chants, each one carrying sound frequencies meant to trigger the pineal gland and facilitate connection to other dimensions. It is safest in the hands of a brāhmaṇa who follows dharma, as his body will only connect to the higher sattvic realms. But when a person of a low frequency with intentions to control others or cause harm uses it (for e.g., in vaśīkaraṇa), it can be detrimental to society at large.

Women of menstrual age and the śūdra varṇa, owing to their low vibrational frequency, are the easiest targets for vaśīkaraṇa, using entities from low dimensions. It is for this reason and for protection from these unpleasant experiences that the śūdra is advised to always be in service of a brāhmaṇa. This injunction was obviously not for the physical protection of the śūdra man, who is often bigger and more muscular than a brāhmaṇa. The protection that the brāhmaṇa offers is by virtue of his high vibrational aura, which disturbance causing low realm beings cannot penetrate due to the mismatch in frequencies.

Similarly, it is time to set right the misinterpretation of Manu (XI.9.3)[91] and other texts which say that women are to be protected by their father or brother before marriage and by their husband and son after marriage. It is not the physical protection that is meant here. So, there is no point in teaching young girls kung fu and karate in defiance of Manu.

In the name of fighting for the rights of women of menstrual age and the śūdra varṇa, making them perform the karma of the other varṇa-s is detrimental to the individuals involved and to society at

---

91 पिता रक्षति कौमारे भर्ता रक्षति यौवने । रक्षन्ति स्थविरे पुत्रा न स्त्री स्वातन्त्र्यमर्हति ॥ ३ ॥

'Her father guards her during virginity, the husband guards her in youth, the sons guard her in old age; the woman should not be left to be independent.' – Manu (IX.9.3). (The dependence is also with reference to not being eligible to read/recite chants themselves.) This is also mentioned in Mahābhārata (13.46.14), Baudhāyana (2-3.45), Vaśiṣṭha (5.3), Viṣṇu (25.13), Yājñavalkya (1.85-86), Nārada (Vivādaratnākara, p. 410), etc.

large. Even in the case where women or the śūdra varṇa are made to officiate as temple arcaka-s, it would be prudent to ensure that it is for a deity who is of a vibrational frequency that the arcaka's body can handle. For example, in the testimonial of the brahmacārini in chapter one, she was made to perform abhiṣeka seva to Meenakshi Amma, who is a high vibration śānta rūpa (peaceful form) of Devī. Moreover, she was asked to do the alaṅkāra during menstruation, which should have been avoided at all costs.[92] What happened to her is very likely a direct consequence of these actions, although unknowingly done and with good intentions.

To prevent such incidents, in all cases where women and the śūdra varṇa are made to officiate as arcaka-s, it would be wise to remain mindful of any changes in the arcaka's physical or mental health. If this happens, along with sudden accidents or negative incidents in the vicinity of the temple or to the arcaka, it would be better to conduct a Deva Praśnam[93] to understand the changes that might have occurred in the caitanya of the temple and undertake the necessary corrections as per the śāstra-s.

Varṇa of non-humans

If varṇa is not just a social classification based on a human being's occupation and is instead about a subtle vibrational

---

92 The reasons why women should not enter temples during menstruation is explained in detail in the author's earlier book - Rtu Vidya.

93 Deva Praśnam is a method of astrology from Kerala, which is used to determine the state of the caitanyam in the temple and the reason for it. In a widely popular online article by Sri Shyamasundara Dasa on 'Ashtamangala Deva Praśnam (copyright 1996), there is a description of how this works. In one of the temples, the reason for the presiding deity Ma Durga's absence and instead the uninvited presence of a fierce form of Ma Kali has been explained. The reason includes sudden death of persons near the community, entry by menstruating women, etc. Source: https://shyamasundaradasa.com/jyotish/resources/articles/adp/ashtamangala_deva_prasna_1.html

quality, it should extend beyond humans as well. After all, matter in different forms is fundamentally just the manifestation of different frequencies of vibration. If this is really how the ṛṣi-s of Bhārat understood varṇa, then they should have mentioned such a vibrational division in the plant and animal kingdom, and even among inanimate objects, isn't it? Do we have such evidence from the ancient texts of Bhārat?

Yes, we do! True to the subtle understanding of varṇa, the ṛṣi-s state that there is varṇa even among devatā-s with Agni and Bṛhaspati being considered as the brāhmaṇa among them; Indira, Varuṇā, Soma and Yama as kṣatriya; Vasus, Rudras, Viśvedevā and Maruta as vaiśya; Pusan and Aśvins as śūdra.[94] Regarding trees, the Vṛkṣa Āyurveda speaks about four varṇa-s among wood, describing the brāhmaṇa wood as being light and soft, kṣatriya wood as being light and hard, vaiśya wood as being heavy and soft, and śūdra wood as being heavy and hard.[95] Similarly, if we look at the danda (staff) given to each of the dvija-s during upanayana, we see that the danda is to be made of a different tree for each varṇa, with palāśa (flame of the forest) for the brāhmaṇa, aśvatthā (fig tree) for the kṣatriya and the audumbara (udumbar tree) for the vaiśya varṇa.[96] The classification of animals as per varṇa is detailed along the same lines as the puruṣa sūkta in the Jaiminīya Brāhmaṇa, with the goat being of brāhmaṇa, the horse of kṣatriya, cow of vaiśya, and sheep of śūdra varṇa.[97] Bṛhat Saṃhita, in the section on Ratna Parīkṣā (examination of gems), mentions the four-fold classification of diamonds with white diamond being for

---

94 Maitrayāni Saṃhita I.10.13, Śatapatha 14.4.2.23-25, Śāntiparva 208.23-35

95 Vriksha Ayurveda - लघु यत् कोमलं काष्ठं सुघटं ब्रह्मजाति तत् । दृढागं लघु यत् काष्ठमघटं क्षत्रजाति तत् ॥ कोमलं गुरु यत् काष्ठं वैश्यजाति तदुच्यते । दृढागं गुरु यत् काष्ठं शूद्रजाति तदुच्यते

96 Voice of God, Vol 2, chapter 'Qualities of a brahmacharin.'

97 Jaiminīya Brāhmaṇa, 1.68 - 9

brāhmaṇa, red or yellow for kṣatriya, yellow for vaiśya and black for śūdra.[98, 99]

Thus, we see that varṇa, as the frequency of vibration and the resulting aura, is a subtle and correct understanding of the word and its usage, which will uncover the meaning behind many of the injunctions in the śāstra-s that would otherwise seem meaningless or strange. When a particular theory on varṇa is able to answer many of the rules prescribed in the śāstra-s pertaining to varṇa, it means that the theory applied is an understanding in the right direction.

---

98 Brihat Samhita, Chapter 80, Ratna Pariksha

99 The different frequencies within a varṇa (eg., animal, plant, etc.) should probably be understood as multiples of a fundamental frequency, through the concept of harmonics.

Chapter 5: Upanayana Saṃskāra

A deeper understanding of the upanayana saṃskāra is needed if we are to properly decode the rules for women and the śūdra varṇa. Such an understanding should enable us to satisfactorily answer the following questions, which relate to the śāstra rules on this subject, covered in chapter two.

- What is the purpose of upanayana saṃskāra?

- Why is upanayana not encouraged in the same way for women and the śūdra varṇa, as it is done for the other three varṇa-s?

- What is the purpose of wearing the yajñopavita, and has it been prescribed for women?

The śāstra-s state that before upanayana, there are no strict rules for a child, and regardless of the family he is born into, he is considered a śūdra until he undergoes the upanayana saṃskāra. This is because it is through the upanayana saṃskāra that a child obtains the eligibility to start the spiritual journey and is given the means to activate the dormant spiritual tendencies. When a child is initiated either by his father or a paṇḍit, during upanayana, he gets inducted into the gotra of his ancestors, and his ātma is able to restart his journey towards mokṣa. We find examples of even avatars such as Śrī Rāma, Śrī Kṛṣṇa and Śrī Dattatreya (in his avatar as Śri Narasimha Saraswati) having undergone the upanayana ceremony before commencing the purpose of their avatar. Once the ātma takes a human birth as a male in any of the first three varṇa-s, it is only through the upanayana ceremony that their connection to the gotra is established. It is only when this connection is made to the gotra that the blessings of the ṛṣi-s of that gotra and of pitṛ-s (ancestors) flow through.

So, we see that the upanayana ceremony awakens the spiritual tendency that lies dormant until that point. Where are these spiritual tendencies stored? What is actually getting activated in this process? What is it that connects the dvija men to a gotra?

The answer to all these questions is the 'Y' chromosome. The human male is born with a single X and a single Y chromosome. The human female is born with two X chromosomes, and there is no Y chromosome in the biological female. This is the primary differentiating factor. The connection to one's gotra is actually a subtle awakening of the ādhyātmika saṃskāra (spiritual tendencies) in the Y chromosome. The biological males in a gotra, by virtue of possessing the Y chromosome, are capable of receiving the spiritual abilities of that gotra. The ṛṣi-s in a gotra and one's ancestors (pitṛ-s) are linked by the Y chromosome, and hence, all subtle communication via rituals happens through a male who has been initiated via upanayana. The initiation into the Gāyatrī mantra during the upanayana ceremony is what strengthens the Y-chromosome's subtle spiritual abilities.

Even if we consider the non-spiritual aspects, the regular chanting of the Gāyatrī mantra is what can help boys manage the surge and play of testosterone. The Gāyatrī mantra, when chanted regularly, triggers the ājña cakra and, therefore, the pituitary gland. The pituitary gland causes the release of the hormone testosterone. While this male hormone plays an important role in the reproductive health functions of boys and men, it is also responsible for sexual tendencies and aggressive behaviour if not controlled or channelled properly. The ability to practice self-restraint and self-control is possible when the prefrontal cortex (in the forehead) is activated.[100,101] Without an active prefrontal cortex, the production of testosterone could lead to aggressive and hyper-sexual behaviour. Through the practice of brahmacārya and chanting of the Gāyatrī mantra, the prefrontal cortex is activated, and boys are better able to manage the surge of testosterone, in addition to starting their spiritual journey.

Age for Upanayana

Śāstra-s mention the age of 7 to 8 years from conception for brāhmaṇa, 11 for kṣatriya and 12 for vaiśya varṇa, for the upanayana saṃskāra. If this age is missed, then the upper limit for each of the three varṇa-s is given as 16, 22 and 24 years, respectively. Let us see why this might be necessary.

Studies indicate that, on average, there is little testosterone (<1 nmol/L) found in males before the age of 10 years, at which point the levels begin to rise. Between 10 and 15 years of age, plasma testosterone levels increase nearly seven-fold. The rate of increase slows as the males reach adult levels (~15 nmol/L) between the ages of 16 and 17 years. Looking at the data from the study, we find that the total testosterone levels at the age of around 10 years were found to be 0.72 nmol/L, at the age of around 11-12 years as 1.47 nmol/L, and then it suddenly jumps to 6.87 nmol/L at age 13 years.[102]

---

100 Knoch, Daria and Fehr Ernst. Resisting the Power of Temptations: The Right Prefrontal Cortex and Self-Control. Ann. N.Y. Acad. Sci. 1104: 123–134 (2007). C 2007 New York Academy of Sciences. doi: 10.1196/annals.1390.00

101 Berkovich-Ohana A, Wilf M, Kahana R, Arieli A, Malach R. Repetitive speech elicits widespread deactivation in the human cortex: the "Mantra" effect? Brain Behav. 2015 Jul;5(7):e00346. doi: 10.1002/brb3.346. Epub 2015 May 4

102 Khairullah A, Klein LC, Ingle SM, May MT, Whetzel CA, Susman EJ, Paus T. Testosterone trajectories and reference ranges in a large longitudinal sample of male adolescents. PLoS One. 2014 Sep 30;9(9):e108838. doi: 10.1371/journal.pone.0108838. PMID: 25268961; PMCID: PMC4182562.

From the above data, it can be understood that the early initiation of a brāhmaṇa child was in keeping with the svadharma of pursuing the study of Veda-s and performance of various rituals requiring connection to devatā-s and pitṛ-s, for which absolute control of testosterone (and resulting impulses) is needed. Therefore, the age for initiation is before the biological rise of testosterone in the body, so that the ability to practice self-restraint is cultivated early.

The age of 11 for the kṣatriya varṇa, and the age of 12 for the vaiśya varṇa seems to allow leeway to cultivate tendencies required for their respective svadharma. This is explained in the Āpastamba Gṛhya Sūtra (I.I.I) thus: 'A person desirous of excellence in sacred learning (should undergo upanayana) in his seventh year, a person desirous of long life in his eighth year, a person desirous of manly vigour in his ninth year, a person desirous of food in his tenth year, a person desirous of strength in his eleventh year, a person desirous of cattle in his twelfth year.'

In any case, for all three varṇa-s the ideal age of initiation should be before 13 years, when there would be a sudden surge in testosterone, thereby making it difficult to get early control over one's testosterone-driven impulses.

Upanayana restrictions for the śūdra varṇa

In the previous chapters, we have explored how the śūdra varṇa is not encouraged to chant Vedic mantra-s because their body is discordant by nature and has a low vibrational capacity. A study on meditation naïve volunteers using EEG and FMRI to study brain activity found that 'for novice meditators, restlessness can arise due to continuous listening to the Gāyatrī mantra.'[103] This was

---

103 Thomas, Susan and Rao, Shobini. Effect of Gayatri Mantra Meditation on Meditation Naive Subjects: an EEG and fMRI Pilot Study. The International Journal of Indian Psychology ISSN 2348-5396 (e) | ISSN: 2349-3429 (p) Volume 3, Issue 2, No.7, DIP: 18.01.115/20160302, ISBN: 978-1-329-92551-9. January - March, 2016

understood in a comprehensive way by the ṛṣi-s, who formulated rules for the śūdra varṇa's protection. Therefore, there is no need for upanayana, which is meant to initiate men into Gāyatrī chanting and Vedic study. Instead, the śūdra varṇa is encouraged to practice seva and bhakti as an alternative. There are many exceptions recorded in the purāṇa-s of people of the śūdra varṇa who had siddhi-s by virtue of surrendering to the divine while adhering to their svadharma. One such example is the story of a butcher (Dharmavyādha) from the Mahābharata, which is given in the chapter titled 'Exceptions.'

So, it is possible for the śūdra varṇa to attain mokṣa, but through the means of complete bhakti and seva, while following their svadharma. Upanayana or Vedic mantra chanting is not needed in the case of the śūdra and will cause them physical and mental problems if done.

Upanayana restrictions for women

Upanayana is undertaken to awaken the dormant Y chromosome. The Y chromosome is naturally absent in a biological female at birth. However, women do receive the Y chromosome through sexual intercourse.[104] A recent (2012) study found that male semen contains a protein called 'sex peptide', which acts as a master regulator when it enters the female bloodstream. This means that the male protein brings about a number of changes in the female genetic makeup. The study stated that a total of 335 differentially regulated genes were identified in females, with 190 genes upregulated and 145 genes downregulated, following seminal fluid

---

104 Chomont, Nicolas, et al. Detection of Y Chromosome DNA as Evidence of Semen in Cervicovaginal Secretions of Sexually Active Women. Journal for American Society for Micobiology. 1 Sep 2001. DOI: https://doi.org/10.1128/cdli.8.5.955-958.2001

contact.[105] Another study came up with a unique finding that male microchimerism[106] in the human female brain is relatively frequent (positive in 63% of subjects), distributed in multiple brain regions, and is potentially persistent across the human lifespan (the oldest female in whom male DNA was detected in the brain was 94 years old).[107] These studies provide evidence that once a woman has received semen through sexual intercourse, the male DNA from her partner remains in her body and even alters her genetic makeup.

What modern scientists are only now beginning to learn was known to the ancient ṛṣi-s ages ago. It is in recognition of this biological fact that the ṛṣi-s prescribed vivāha saṃskāra as the equivalent of upanayana for women, and women's gotra and kula are said to become that of her husband's post marriage. The transfer of semen without the rituals of vivāha is not considered valid for the initiation of a child born out of wedlock. Just as upanayana rituals make a boy eligible by activating the dormant Y chromosome, vivāha rituals play a similar role for women by preparing them spiritually. Without vivāha, women remain uninitiated in the spiritual path. That is why the śāstra-s do not permit a male child born out of wedlock to be initiated into upanayana, even though both his parents might be of any of the first three varṇa-s. Also, it is only after the first sexual intercourse (without protection), post vivāha saṃskāra, that the wife's gotra and kula are said to have changed to that of her husband's. The time advised for the first sexual intercourse after vivāha is different in different sampradāyā-s, and so we see that according to Aśvalāyana Gṛhya Sūtra (I.8.12), the change in kula & gotra happens one year after marriage, while Laghu Hārita says

---

105 The Female Response to Seminal Fluid. John E. Schjenken and Sarah A. Robertson. 17 APR 2020 https://doi.org/10.1152/physrev.00013.2018

106 Microchimerism is the presence of cells from one individual in another genetically distinct individual.

107 Chan WF, Gurnot C, Montine TJ, Sonnen JA, Guthrie KA, Nelson JL. Male microchimerism in the human female brain. PLoS One. 2012;7(9):e45592. doi: 10.1371/journal.pone.0045592. Epub 2012 Sep 26. PMID: 23049819; PMCID: PMC3458919.

it happens immediately after marriage, etc.[108] In any case, if a woman has conceived post vivāha saṃskāra, it is a confirmation that her gotra and kula have become that of her husband.

This insight will also help us understand why the ancient texts talk about men having more than one wife but why women were never encouraged to have more than one husband. If a woman marries more than one man, each time, her body undergoes genetic modifications (after sexual union). In the case of Draupadi, too, we find that even though she married five men, they were brothers who were of the same gotra. In the case of women whose husbands were infertile, the śāstra-s recommended that they could conceive through their husband's biological brother or another sagotra (same gotra) person.[109] This was called conceiving through niyoga.[110]

While men are connected to their gotra through upanayana saṃskāra and receive Vedic education from a Guru, women receive the benefits of the spiritually strengthened Y-chromosome by tuning in to their husband, considering him as a Guru. Vivāha rituals, when done properly, connect the husband and wife in a way as a Guru is connected to his śiṣya (disciple). Thus, the spiritual path for a woman unfolds naturally after vivāha saṃskāra and through the blessings of her husband. Needless to say, the husband's spiritual quotient directly influences the ease or difficulty with which the wife can progress in her spiritual journey.

When women completely surrender their aham in the seva of their husband, it is called Pativratā Dharma. We might tend to

---

108 Vide Dr. P.V. Kane, History of Dharmaśāstra, Vol II, Part 1, Chapter IX.

109 Apastambha Dharmasutra (II.10 27.2-4) – 'One shall not make over (his wife) to strangers (for a son by niyoga) but only to one who is a sagotra.

110 In the case of niyoga, such relationships were approved by the husband and were only for the sake of conceiving, and the woman continued to stay with her husband. Note that the dharmaśāstra's say that Niyoga is not prescribed during kali yuga owing to people's inability to practice restraint and weakness of the senses.

take it very lightly, but do note that pativratā dharma is what is responsible for Sitā, Draupadī, Lopamudrā, Anasūyā and other women mentioned in the Veda-s and upaniṣad's gaining their siddhi-s; not Vedic study as is usually presumed. When pativratā dharma is perfected through a complete surrender of aham, an inner transformation occurs. If the husband also follows his spiritual path as guided by his guru, then the wife, through devotion to the husband, merges with him energetically. This manifests as the two intuitively feeling and experiencing each other naturally, while internally, each experiences the divine masculine and feminine within themselves. This is the Ardhanārīśvara form — when both husband and wife have attained a high state of spiritual progress and a sense of oneness with each other. The form of Ardhanārīśvara is said to be realised at the Viśuddhi cakra (base of the throat). The Viśuddhi is considered the mokṣa dvār, and raising one's awareness to this cakra is crucial for the next step towards mokṣa.

While men can reach this stage through yoga sādhanā, even on their own (without marriage), since they biologically possess both the X and Y chromosomes, for women, marriage becomes an essential step for such a possibility to occur. Therefore, women becoming brahmacārini-s or sannyasin-s was generally not encouraged in Sanātana Dharma.

Brahmacārya for girls

One of the śāstra texts[111] states that brahmacārya for girls lasts only until the 10th or 12th year (before menarche). Do note that brahmacārya is here thought of as a biological state for girls, unlike its consideration as a practice of celibacy for boys. Understanding this difference is crucial. Brahmacārya is the phase where the human seed is not released from the body and is instead held within. In boys,

---

111 दशवार्षिकं ब्रह्मचर्यं कुमारीणां द्वादशवार्षिकं वा । लौगाक्षगृह 19. 2 Laugāksi Gr. (19.2), vide Dr. P.V. Kane, 'History of Dharmaśāstra', Vol II, Part 1,

they would have to practice celibacy to withhold the seed (which is otherwise released with semen) and follow the spiritual practices prescribed to transform it into subtler forms (ojas and tejas). The chanting of Gāyatrī mantra by boys aids in this process.

In girls, all through the menstrual years, they have no control over the seed (egg) as it is involuntarily released during menstruation. Therefore, only the years before the first period (menarche) is considered as the phase of brahmacārya for girls. With this understanding, we should note that even if girls or women practice celibacy, it does not serve the same purpose as they lose the seed (egg) every month during menstruation. On the other hand, if they take up spiritual practices that work on transforming the seed, then the withholding of the seed will result in a stoppage of menstruation, thereby affecting their overall health. Further, if women chanted the Gāyatrī mantra regularly, their testosterone levels would shoot up and cause menstrual and reproductive difficulties. When we understand this biologically, it will become obvious why women could not have been initiated into Vedic chanting, Gāyatrī mantra or brahmacārya in the same way as the dvija men.

Interestingly, one of the verses quoted to defend the idea that girls were also initiated into Vedic study is a description of the Samāvartana ceremony, which is done by students at the end of their study period. In Āśvalāyana Gṛhya Sutra III.8, in the ceremony of Samāvartana, on the subject of applying ointment, it says:[112]

> अनुलेपनेन पाणी प्रलिप्य मुखमग्रे ब्राह्मणोऽनुलिम्पेत् । बाहू राजन्यः ।
> उदरं वैश्यः । उपस्थं स्त्री । ऊरू सरणजीविनः । आश्व. गृ. III. 8. 11.

> 'After having smeared the two hands with ointment, a brāhmaṇa should salve his face first, a kṣatriya his two hands, a vaiśya his belly, a woman her genitals, and persons who gain their livelihood by running, their thighs.'

---

112 Vide 'History of Dharmaśāstra' by Dr. P.V.Kane.

Here, we find that the part of the body that each type of student anoints is that which is vibrationally a match to their varṇa. Also, the mantra-s given and the Veda studied were suitable to his vibration. So, in the case of girls, even if she was made to study the Veda-s or chant mantra-s, it is likely that she was taught verses pertaining to the lower part of the body (such as for reproductive health). In the Mahābhārata (Vānaparva 305.20), a brāhmaṇa is said to have taught the mother of the pāṇḍava-s a number of mantra-s from Atharvaśiras. The Atharva Veda is generally not studied by the first three varṇa-s, and if done, it is done as a secondary study after finishing the study of the Veda, which is recommended by his gotra. The Atharva Veda is at times said to be similar to tantra in terms of it consisting of low-frequency mantra-s that can be used by all varṇa-s and also by women after initiation. If that is the case, it can be understood that these low-frequency mantra-s might have been taught to girls or women in this particular sampradāya. Further, it would have been taught only for a short time before menarche, as Hārita says that in the case of girls, Samāvartana took place before the appearance of menses - प्राग्रजसः समावर्तनम् । इति हारीतोक्त्या - संस्कारप्रकाश p. 404.

In general, the śāstra-s do not say that the path of the brahmacāriṇi would help women attain svarga. Instead, the śāstra-s have repeatedly stated that it is vivāha and pativratā dharma that is the prescribed path for women to attain siddhi-s and svarga. This is evident in several verses from different śāstra-s and purāṇa-s, a few of which are given below:[113]

असंस्कृतायाः कन्यायाः कुतो लोकास्तवानघे । शल्यपर्व 52. 12.

'In the Śalyaparva chapter 52, we have the story of a girl, daughter of Kuṇi Garga, who practised severe penance till she reached old age and yet was told by Nārada that if she died unmarried, she would not attain svarga. Therefore, the

---

113 Vide 'History of Dharmaśāstra' by Dr. P.V. Kane

woman induced Śṛngavat of the Gālava family for a day prior to her death to marry her by the promise of giving him half of the puṇya she earns.'

Similarly, we see that even at the time of the unexpected death of a girl, a ritual was performed if she was unmarried.

तथैव कन्यां च मृतां प्राप्तयौवनां तुल्येन पुंसा प्राप्तगृहवत्तां दहेत् । वैखानस- स्मार्तसूत्र V. 9.

The Vaikhānasa Smārta Sūtra (V.9), while describing the ceremony of funeral rites in case of distress, mentions the practice of finding a male of the same varṇa for a girl who dies unmarried though of the age of puberty, with whom a sort of marriage is gone through, and the girl is then cremated.

In Yama, it is explicitly stated that neither in the Veda-s nor in the dharmaśāstra-s, is pravrajyā (an ascetic's life) enjoined for women; (procreation and care of) a progeny from a male of the same varṇa as herself is her proper dharma. This is the established rule.[114]

यत्तु यमेनोक्तं स्त्रियाः श्रुतौ वा शास्त्रे वा प्रव्रज्या न विधीयते । प्रजा हि तस्याः स्वो धर्मः सवर्णादिति धारणा ॥ प्रव्रज्या ब्रह्मचर्यमित्यर्थः । स्मृतिच. (व्यवहार P. 254).

In the Śri Guru Caritra too, a woman named Savitri, whose dead husband was brought back to life by Gurunath, asks Gurunath to give her mantrōpadeśa to protect her and her husband against all turmoils of life, to give them a safe passage to life beyond and to liberate them forever. Gurunath told her that for a woman, no mantra is needed. It is only patiseva that is needed for a woman, and this alone would safely ferry her across the ocean of saṃsāra to the heavenly shores beyond. He told her that for a woman, mantra is not as efficacious as patiseva. He also shares the story of how the Sanjeevani mantra's

---

114 Yama quoted in Smṛti Candrika (on vyavahāra p. 254) Vide 'History of Dharmaśāstra' by Dr. P.V. Kane, Volume II, Part II, Ch. XXVIII, Page 945

potency was lost because it was given to a woman. As Gurunath thus dissuaded Savitri from being desirous of taking a mantra, the woman pleaded that she be taught some vrata, which would be as beneficial as a mantra. That is when Gurunath taught her about the Somavara Śiva Vrata. All of this is described in the Śrī Guru Caritra, Chapter 35.

These are not mere stories but important concepts shared in a way that a common person can grasp. These stories have to be taken as seriously as the dharmaśāstra injunctions.

Yajñopavīta

The name for the sacred thread worn by the first three varṇa-s following upanayana is actually upavīta, which also means upper garment. It is also called brahmasūtra in some of the ancient texts (Yaj. I.16). When it is worn in the way for the performance of yajña/homa, it is called yajñopavīta. An important question in the minds of many Hindu-s is whether or not girls/women were made to wear the sacred thread. In order to answer this question, we should be able to understand the purpose of the sacred thread worn in different ways. Let us begin by understanding the three ways in which it is worn.

One of the earliest mentions of yajñopavīta is seen is the Taittiriya Saṃhita II.5.11.1,

निवीतं मनुष्याणां प्राचीनावीतं पितॄणामुपवीतं देवानाम्।

उपव्ययते देवलक्ष्म- मेव तत्कुरुते । तै. सं. II. 5.11.1.

'The nivīta is used (for actions of) men, the prācīnāvīta is used (for rites of) pitṛ-s, the upavīta for devatā-s.'

The wearing of the sacred thread as yajñopavīta and prācīnāvīta is described in Gobhila Gṛhya Sūtra (I.2.2-4),

दक्षिणं बहुमुद्धृत्य शिरोऽवधाय सव्येंऽसे प्रतिष्ठापयति दक्षिणं कक्षमन्ववलम्बं भवत्येवं यज्ञोपवीती भवति । सव्यं बाहुमुद्धृत्य शिरोवधाय दक्षिणेंऽसे प्रतिष्ठापयति । सव्यं कक्षमन्ववलम्बं भवत्येवं

प्राचीनावीती भवति । पितृयज्ञे त्वेवं प्राचीनावीती भवति । गोभिल गृह्य - I. 2. 2-4

'Raising his right arm, putting the head into (the upavīta), he suspends (the cord) over his left shoulder in such a way that it hangs down on his right side; thus he becomes yajñopavītin. Passing his left arm, putting the head (into the upavīta) he suspends it over his right shoulder, so that it hangs down along his left side; in this way he becomes a prācīnāvītin; a person becomes a prācīnāvītin only in the sacrifice offered to the manes (ancestors).'

Regarding the nivīta way of wearing the sacred thread, we have these verses from Baudhāyana Gṛhya Paribhāṣā Sūtra (II.2.3),

उपरिष्टादंसाभ्यां ग्रीवां हृदयं च संपरिगृह्य हृदयस्याधस्तादूर्ध्वं नाभेरङ्गुष्ठाभ्यां परिगृह्णाति तन्निर्वतं मनुष्याणामिति ऋषीणामित्येवेदमुक्तं भवति । अथ निवीतकार्याणि ऋषीणां तर्पणं व्यवसायः प्रजासंस्कारोऽन्यत्र होमात्, मूत्रपुरीषोत्सर्गः प्रेतोद्वहनं यानि चान्यानि मनुष्यकार्याणि कण्ठेऽवसक्तं निवीतमिति । बौ. गृ. परिभाषासूत्र II. 2. 3 and 6.

'When it is carried over the neck, both shoulders and the chest and is held with both the thumbs (of the two hands) lower than the region of the heart and above the navel, that is nivīta. The occasions when nivīta mode is used are: ṛṣi-tarpaṇa, sexual intercourse, saṃskāras of one's children except when homa is to be performed, answering the calls of nature, carrying a corpse and whatever other reasons are meant only for men; nivīta is what hangs from the neck.'

According to Mahāperiyavā, when one is not performing rites to pitṛ-s or performing a homa, the sacred thread has to be worn in the nivīta style (for e.g., during office work in today's times). However, most dvija men today wear it in the yajñopavīta style at all times.

Purpose of wearing the upavīta in three ways

According to Manu,[115] the upavīta for a brāhmaṇa should be made from cotton thread, for a kṣatriya from hemp thread and for a vaiśya from woollen thread. However, in the absence of other materials, Devala says that dvija-s could wear upavīta of cotton, silk, jute, or threadlike portion of the bark of a tree or grass. Today, we see that cotton is what is generally used.

The use of cotton and its being twisted in a specific way such that the strands turn upward (as given in Manu II.2.44) is important to note. Modern science recognises cotton as an excellent acoustic material that achieves multiple effects. Cotton soundproofing materials can absorb, disperse and even contain sound. The natural porosity of cotton helps it absorb and retain sound vibrations. Even a layperson knows through experience that using cotton curtains will reduce the echo in an empty room by absorbing sound.

Therefore, when a cotton thread or garment is worn in a specific way, and then mantra-s are chanted by the wearer (or even listened to from another source), the sound vibrations from the mantra-s are stored in the cotton. Vibrations of sound in the cotton cause the movement of electrons in the atoms of the cotton thread. Movement of electrons in nothing but the flow of current. Thus, when the cotton upavīta is worn in a specific way, there is a subtle flow of current along the thread or garment. Since the thread is twisted upwards, the flow of current will be upwards along the thread when worn as yajñopavīta or prācīnāvīta. When worn as nivīta, the flow of current will be horizontal towards the base of the thread. Whenever there is a

---

115 Manu II. 2.44 states कार्पासमुपवीतं स्याद् विप्रस्यौर्ध्ववृतं त्रिवृत् । शणसूत्रमयं राज्ञो वैश्यस्याविकसौत्रिकम् ॥ ४४ ॥ 'The sacrificial thread worn over the shoulder —which is triple and twisted upwards—should be made of cotton for the brāhmaṇa, of hempen fibres for the kṣatriya, and of woolen fibres for the vaiśya.'—(44)

flow of current, there will be a corresponding magnetic field created. The flow of prāṇa will be greater in the direction of the created magnetic field. If we know the direction of this magnetic field, then we will be able to decipher the purpose of wearing the upavīta in different styles.

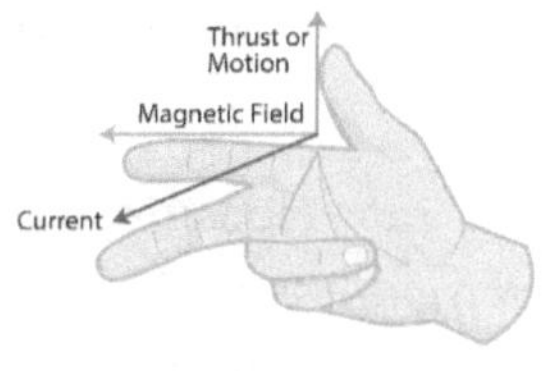

Students of physics will be familiar with Fleming's Right Hand Rule, which can be used to determine the direction of the magnetic field if we know the direction of the current. Fleming's Right Hand Rule states that if we arrange our thumb, forefinger and middle finger of the right hand perpendicular to each other, then the thumb points towards the direction of the motion of the conductor relative to the magnetic field, the forefinger points towards the direction of the magnetic field and the middle finger points towards the direction of the induced current.

Applying this rule, when we place the middle finger of the right hand (representing the current) along the direction of current flow in the upavīta in each mode of wearing it, we find that:

1. In the yajñopavīta style, when the current flows upwards towards the left shoulder, the direction of the magnetic field is outwards and towards the left side of the individual. Thus, the magnetic field energises the Ida Nādi on the left side of the body. According to Swara Yoga,[116] the Ida Nādi is associated with the parasympathetic nervous system and, therefore, triggers the right hemisphere of the brain. The right hemisphere is connected to the left side of the body and is responsible for psychic and extrasensory perception. Therefore, it is this side that must be active during rituals and offerings made to devatā-s.

---

116 Swami Muktibodhananda. Swara Yoga: The Tantric Science of Brain Breathing. 1984

2. In the prācīnāvīta style, when the current flows upwards towards the right shoulder along the thread, we find that the magnetic field represented by the forefinger points directly upwards. Thus, in the prācīnāvīta style, the magnetic field causes the prāṇa to be channelised upwards. This is necessary for the performance of pitṛ rites wherein the communication with pitṛ-s needs to happen from the Sahasrāra cakra at the crown of the head for the subtle offerings to be received properly.

3. In the nivīta style, when current flows horizontally at the base of the thread (located between the heart and navel), the magnetic field points exactly downwards. Thus, the nivīta style channelises prāṇa to the lower part of the body, which is required for physical work, digestion, excretion and other functions pertaining to the lower part of the body.

Upavīta for women

Although we think of the yajñopavīta as a cord of threads, there seems to be evidence that even a cotton garment slung on the left shoulder could act as a yajñopavīta. For example, in Āpastamba Dharmaśāstra (II.2.4.21-22), it says that (a householder) must always wear his garment over (his left shoulder and under his right arm), or he may use a cord only, slung over his left shoulder and passed under his right arm, instead of the garment. Similarly, the Gobhila Gṛhya sūtra (I.2.1), in treating upanayana, says, 'the student takes as yajñopavīta a cord of threads, a garment or a rope of kuśa grass.' The Smṛti Candrika quotes a passage from Ṛṣyaśṛṅga stating, 'One may carry out all the purposes for which yajñopavīta is required by means of a garment and in its absence by a string of three threads.'[117]

---

117 Vide 'History of Dharmaśāstra' by Dr. P.V. Kane, Part I, Vol II, Ch. VII, Page 291

If we take this into consideration, we might understand why, even today, wearing the saree is considered a must for married women who preside over any ritual or homa with their husbands. Most temples that mention the dress code for visiting devotees will insist that women come dressed in a saree. So, wherever women had to wear a yajñopavīta as co-performers of a ritual with their husbands, wearing the saree (especially in the traditional style) was considered the equivalent of the sacred thread. If we understand the purpose of the yajñopavīta as channelling prāṇa towards the left side, the saree's pleated *pallu,* too, would serve the same purpose.

Further, if we look at the nivīta style, going by the functions it performs, we can surmise that it energises the lower part of the body. Therefore, the upavīta for women can be given in the nivīta style at the time of marriage. And indeed, this is what the mangalsūtra is. Hindu women might recollect how the traditional mangalsūtra was as long as the description of the nivīta, was never meant to be removed, and it was to be re-consecrated from time to time, just as men do for the yajñopavīta. A happy confirmation of the above understanding was obtained from the words of Mahāperiyavā, when he said, 'If you ask for an external sign of this (upanayana for women) like the sacred thread worn by men, we may at once point to the married woman's mangalsūtra.'[118]

In some of the sects of the Namboothiri Brāhmaṇa-s of Kerala, even today, there is a ritual where the father of the bride takes three threads of the same length and material as the upavīta meant for men and ties it around his daughter's neck in nivīta style, as part of the vivāha ritual. Like most other rituals which are not understood, this too has become merely symbolic, and women do not wear it after the ritual.[119] Brāhmaṇa-s of Karnataka, Tamil Nadu and Andhra Pradesh,

---

118 Voice of God. Volume 2. Chapter: Upanayana for girls

119 This information has been gathered first-hand by the author, from a Namboothiri Brāhmaṇa who had this ritual performed during his marriage ceremony.

perhaps in understanding of this reluctance by women to wear the cotton thread, decided that it is better that the three threads be added to that of the groom's upavīta with the saṅkalpa that it is for his bride. Thus, we see that married brāhmaṇa men of these regions wear additional threads to their upavīta, after marriage.

Even though the śāstra-s have mentioned that vivāha is the equivalent of upanayana for women, and learned elders often insist that married women should wear their mangalsūtra at all times and dress in a traditional saree, many of us have dismissed these instructions. Instead, we somehow find pleasure in fighting for women's rights for upanayana and yajñopavīta. How silly it all seems when we think about it!

Chapter 6: Agnikriyā

The performance of religious rituals with agni, the sacrificial fire, is generally called agnikriyā. When done on a large scale for the public, it is called a yajña or yāga/yāgam. When done on a smaller scale, it is called a homa or agnihotra. When done at home, after the marriage rites, it is also called aupāsana.

After upanayana, during brahmacārya, while studying the Veda-s, the student performs a daily offering to Agni devatā using sticks of the palāśa (Flame of the Forest) tree. This is called the samidhādhānam. After marriage, when he enters gṛhasthāśrama (order of a householder), he has to perform the daily aupāsana ritual with his wife. He also performs rituals using agni for other devatā-s, and these are the agnihotra rituals, which also require the presence of his wife. When he enters vānaprasthāśrama (becomes a forest recluse), a sacred fire called kakshāgni is prescribed. The sanyasin (renunciate) has no sacrament involving the sacred fire.[120]

Thus, the agnikriya-s involving women are only done after their marriage and require the presence of the woman's husband or a brāhmaṇa (ṛtvik) who can conduct the ritual in the absence of the husband.

Women's Vedic Right

Having witnessed well-meaning organisations encouraging unmarried girls to follow Vedic mantra chanting and teaching women

---

120 Voice of God, Volume 2. Chapter titled 'The importance of Agni.'

to perform agnikriyā by themselves in the name of giving them their Vedic rights, it is important to know what actually are the Vedic rights of women. Quoted below are the words of Mahāperiyavā on giving women back their Vedic rights.[121]

> "Aupāsana begins with marriage and is to be performed every day until one becomes a sannyasin or until one's death. This is done by preserving the sacred fire, which is a witness to the marriage, which is preserved throughout and aupāsana performed in it every day. Even when the husband is away, the wife must offer the akṣata (unbroken rice grains) in the sacrificial fire."

He says that women should fight for this right of theirs and impress upon their husbands the importance of performing aupāsana. Mahāperiyavā says that women should tell their husbands,

> "Even though you have given up all scriptural karma, you at least do the Gāyatrī japa to retain some connection with the Vedic dharma. If you do not do this japa or forget the mantra, sometime in future when you will repent it, you can do it and for that you have at least had upanayana saṃskāra. As for me, I have had no upanayana, nor am I entitled to do Gāyatrī japa. If at all I have been given any right in the Veda-s, it is this aupāsana. If you refuse to perform it, I will be denied my Vedic right."

In this manner, Mahāperiyavā says that women must fight for this sacred right of theirs and make their husbands perform aupāsana. It is also clear from the above that Mahāperiyavā clearly said that Gāyatrī japa is not meant for women.

Mahāperiyavā also stated that though members of the fourth varṇa do not wear the sacred thread, they have the marriage saṃskāra and, along with it, aupāsana, but without the chanting of mantra-s.

121　Voice of God, Volume-2. Chapters titled Aupasana, Aupasana: Women's only Vedic property, The greatness of Agni, Samskaras with Agni

Aupāsana and Agnihotra

It might be useful for us to get a fundamental understanding of the different types of fire sacrifices as ordained in the śāstra-s. What is presented in this section is taken from the words of Mahāperiyavā, as given in the book 'Voice of God' Volume 2, Chapter titled 'Saṃskāra-s with Agni.'[122]

> "Four hundred yajña-s are said to be mentioned in the Veda-s. Of these, aupāsana alone is to be performed by all the four varṇa-s. Though the others can be performed by the first three varṇa-s, it is said that in practice these were performed mostly by brāhmaṇa-s and kṣatriya-s and not much by vaiśya-s. There are yajña-s to be conducted specifically by kṣatriya-s to acquire physical strength, gain victory in war, etc. Similarly, there are yāgā-s that have to be performed by vaiśya-s for a good agricultural yield, for wealth, etc. The yajamāna of a sacrifice might be a person of a kṣatriya or vaiśya varṇa, but the priest/s have to be a brāhmaṇa.[123]

> Any rite meant to fulfil a wish is kāmya-karma, and it comes under the optional category. Then, there are rites that are obligatory and conducted for the good of the other ātman as well as of the world. They come under the category of 'nitya-karma', but the word 'nitya' here does not denote 'daily.'

> In the category of nitya-karma, there are 21 sacrifices. There is no compulsion with regard to the rest of the 400. But the 21 included in the forty saṃskāra-s must be performed at

---

122 For more details, please refer to the book 'Voice of God' Volume 2, English Translation.

123 From the understanding of the vibrational frequency of brāhmaṇa varṇa, we should note that only through the brāhmaṇa varṇa can the high frequency deities be contacted and offering made to them.

least once in a lifetime. These are divided into groups of seven: pākayajña, haviryajña and somayajña.

Marriage is conducted with offerings made in the fire. The aupāsana rite, which must be performed every day, is commenced with this fire, and it must be preserved throughout one's life. The seven pākayajña-s, upanayana and śrāddhā must be performed in this aupāsana fire. The son lights his aupāsana fire during his marriage from his father's aupāsana fire, and it must be maintained throughout his life. Thus, without a break, the sacred fire is kept burning in the family from generation to generation.

All rites in which the aupāsana fire is used and pertain to an individual and his family are gṛhyakarma-s. The gṛhya-sūtra texts deal with such rites. They belong to the smṛti-s and are called smārta-karmas. The elaborate rites that are specifically meant for the well-being of mankind are called śrauta-karma because their procedure is directly based on the authority of the śruti, or the Veda-s. The śāstra-s dealing with them are śrauta-sūtra.

The fire of the aupāsana (done at the time of marriage and taken from that of the groom's father) is divided into two in a ceremony called 'agniādhānam.' One part is called the 'gruhyāgni' or 'smārthāgni': it is meant for rites performed at home called smārta-karma. The second part is 'srauthāgni' and is meant for śrauta rites. These two sacred fires must be preserved throughout. Gruhyāgni is also called the aupāsana agni since the daily rites of aupāsana are to be performed in it. Similarly, agnihotra (oblation to fire) is a śrauta ceremony and it too must be performed twice a day. If the agnihotra fire is extinguished for whatever reason, it must be kindled again through a new ādhānam ceremony. The same applies for aupāsana fire.

In aupāsana, unbroken rice grains are offered in the fire, and in agnihotra either milk or ghee or unbroken rice grains (are offered)."

Mahāperiyavā says that the sacred fire must be kept burning by adding rice husk to it every now and then and that this aupāsana fire will keep away all evil spirits and afflictions of all types. He says that wearing the aupāsana ashes is a great protection.

In an earlier chapter, it was mentioned that women and the śūdra varṇa, owing to their low vibrational frequency, often tend to attract and become prey to other's negative thoughts (dṛṣṭi) and negative intentions (vāmācāra). The sacred ash from the aupāsana agni is one of the ways to protect themselves against these.

Source of agni and pañcayajña

What really needs to register in our mind is that the agni used for the rituals performed by a householder of the first three varṇa-s should necessarily be the same agni which was witness to his marriage ritual. It is only the śūdra varṇa who can use ordinary fire for aupāsana.

In addition to the words of Mahāperiyavā, the following verses from Manu (III.67), Yājñavalkya (1.97), Viṣṇu (59.1-3), Baudhāyana (2.2.75), etc.[124] make this very clear.

---

124 Yājñavalkya (1.97).—'The Householder should every day perform the Smārta-rites in the marriage-fire, or in the fire installed at the time of succession to property; and the Śrauta rites are to be performed in the Śrauta Fire.'

Viṣṇu (59.1-3).—'The Householder shall perform the Pākayajñas in the Marriage-Fire; also the Agnihotra, both morning and evening; he shall also pour libations to the Gods.'

Baudhāyana (2.2.75).—'The installation of Fire begins with marriage; in that should the rites be performed till such time as the regular Laying of the Fire.'

Manu III.67:

वैवाहिकेऽग्नौ कुर्वीत गृह्यं कर्म यथाविधि ।

पञ्चयज्ञविधानं च पक्तिं चान्वाहिकीं गृही ॥ ६७ ॥

In the marriage-fire the householder should perform the gṛhya rites; as also the rite of the five sacrifices (pañcayajña) and the daily cooking.—(67)

The pañcamahāyajña-s ordained for all gṛhasta-s (householders) are brahmayajña (chanting of the Veda), deva yajña (sacrifices and pūjā), pitṛ yajña (tarpaṇa), manuṣya yajña (feeding guests) and bhūta yajña (offering bali to various creatures).

The ritual of bhūta yajña is also called Vaiśvadeva, in which offerings (bali) are made in the fire, or they are placed inside and outside the house with the chanting of mantra-s. Here too, women and the śūdra varṇa can offer the bali, but without mantra-s (as given in the śāstra injunctions mentioned in chapter two).

The śūdra varṇa is also entitled to perform the mahāyajña-s in the ordinary fire; he could perform śrāddhā, he was to think of the devatā-s and utter loudly the word 'namaḥ' which was to be the only mantra in his case (i.e. he was not to say 'agnaye svāhā) but to think of agni and say namaḥ.[125]

Although the śūdra was not to perform Vedic rites or read the Veda-s, he was entitled to perform what is called pūrta-dharma, i.e. the building of wells, tanks, temples, parks and distribution of food as works of charity and gifts on such occasion as eclipses and the Sun's passage from one zodiacal sign into another and on the 12th and other tithis.[126] Further, for the śūdra varṇa, since vivāha rites are not performed with mantra-s, they did not have to preserve the vaivāhika

---

125 Gau.10.66-67, laghuvishnu V.9, Vishnu Purana III.8.33; Santiparva 60.37-38:

126 Atri Verse 46: इष्टापूर्तौ द्विजातीनां सामान्यौ धर्मसाधनौ । अधिकारी भवेच्छूद्रः पूर्तधर्मे न वैदिके।।

agni and could use the ordinary fire for aupāsana rituals, which also has to be done without mantra-s. [127]

Agnihotra

There are numerous studies with data which provide evidence of the perceptible environmental and health impact of performing agnihotra and yajña. One extensive study[128] has shown that performing agnihotra considerably reduced the microbial load in the air for up to 30 feet, enhanced plant growth, the levels of NO_2 in the surrounding atmosphere increased from 0.0086 ppm to 0.0094 ppm due to agnihotra fumes and SO_2 levels in the atmosphere reduced from 1.44 ppm to 0.56 ppm due to agnihotra fumes (performed at sunset). On the benefits of agnihotra ash, the same study found that agnihotra ash can be used to treat skin ailments effectively and can also be used as a plant fertiliser as it promotes the germination of seeds. Another aspect of this study found the ability of the agnihotra ash to neutralise the genotoxic effect, reducing bacterial load and purifying water. Another source[129] has explained in detail the chemical changes occurring due to the use of specific ingredients during a yajña.

What is lesser known or discussed is the subtler aspects of agni — why is it considered as a sākṣī (witness) and as a vehicle to carry offerings to devatā-s and pitṛ-s. Why is there the rule that most of the agnikriyā-s are only to be performed by married men wearing a sacred thread and a śikhā (tuft of hair on the crown of the head)? The

---

127 Mitakshara on Yaj I.121 say that the śūdra should offer oblations in the ordinary fire and that there is no Vaivāhika fire for the śūdra.

128 Pathade, Girish & Abhang, Pranay. (2014). Scientific study of Vedic Knowledge Agnihotra. Bharatiya Bouddhik Sampada: A Quarterly Science Research Journal of Vijñāna Bharati. 43-44. 18-27.

129 Pt. Shriram Sharma Acarya, 'The Integrated Science of Yajna.' Compiled by Dr. Ranjani Joshi, IIT Mumbai. Publisher Shantikunj, Haridwar. First Edition 2001

fact that they should be married implies a significant role played by their wife; what might that be?

Agni as sākṣī

Agni is often considered as a sākṣī (witness), and all-important Vedic rituals are therefore performed in the presence of agni. Being a witness means understanding that agni possesses intelligence and memory. The importance placed on the vaivāhika agni, which becomes the basis of all smārta and śrauta rites for a householder of the first three varṇa-s, indicates that the ancient ṛṣi-s seemed to have understood some subtle phenomena regarding agni, which we have not yet fully recognised. Let us explore what that might be.

Fire has the properties of heat and light. Heat is responsible for the increased temperature, which causes the atoms in the air around the fire to vibrate at high energy and thus release electrons. The loose electrons increase the overall negative charge in the air near the fire. A negative charge is considered conducive to good health and immunity. To this, if one adds specific offerings such as unbroken rice during aupāsana, the resulting chemical reaction will cleanse and purify the air. This much benefit from daily aupāsana is available even for those who are not eligible to chant mantra-s.

Chanting mantra-s into the fire causes the atoms to vibrate at the specific frequency of the mantra, thereby carrying the added benefit of specific sound frequencies to the negatively charged electrons. Each time the electron undergoes excitation (jumps to a higher energy level) based on the sound frequency or light energy received, it emits a photon corresponding to the energy loss during de-excitation (returning to its stationary state) of that electron. Also, when light strikes the copper plate of the agni-kunda, which is shaped like an inverted pyramid, there will be a continuous release of photons due to the photoelectric effect.[130]

---

130 One can study the photoelectric effect and electron transition states of Hydrogen atom, to know more about electron excitation and de-excitation.

A photon is a particle of light, which essentially is a packet of electromagnetic radiation. Very recently, photons of light have been attributed with memory called 'quantum memory', and this is being used in advanced quantum computing. According to a 2020 study,[131] the simplest way to get photons compatible with atomic-based quantum memory is to generate the photons from a system of the same atoms. Could this perhaps be the reason why agni is called a sākṣī and the same vaivāhika agni is to be preserved and used for all subsequent agnikriyā-s?

There is another interesting quantum theory that might tickle our minds while contemplating the need for a man to be linked to his wife for the performance of fire rituals. This is the theory of quantum entanglement and quantum teleportation, which in 2022 won the Nobel Prize. The theory of entanglement says that when two particles (could be photons, qubits, cells, molecules, etc.) are in entanglement, what happens to one simultaneously happens to the other, even if they are physically apart. Two entangled particles make up a whole, and when measured, each particle will have the same but opposite value of the other. For example, if one entangled particle was found to have a spin up, the other one would be found to have a spin down because the two together make a full zero spin. In physics, it takes a bit of work to create photons that are entangled (e.g., a laser beam is passed through a crystal, which then emits two photons, etc). But in a biological body, if we remove two cells from the same source, they will already be in an entangled state.

The śāstra-s time and again mention that after vivāha, the husband and wife become one half of each other. Perhaps this is what Sitā, too, had meant when she spoke about how things changed after circumambulating the agni with her husband Rām. When Sitā met a

---

131 Ma L, Slattery O, Tang X. Optical Quantum Memory and its Applications in Quantum Communication Systems. J Res Natl Inst Stand Technol. 2020 Jan 16;125:125002. doi: 10.6028/jres.125.002. PMID: 35646477; PMCID: PMC9119665.

female sage, the sage said to Sitā, "It is a great blessing to be perfectly obedient to such a husband as Rām; you are that. You must be happy." To this, Sitā replied saying:

> "Mother, I do not know whether I obey him or he obeys me. One thing alone I remember that when he took me by the hand before the sacrificial fire — whether it was a reflection of the fire or whether God himself made it appear to me — I found that I was his and he was mine. And since then, I have found that I am the compliment of his life, and he of mine."[132]

Those who have experienced such 'entangled states' with their partner would have experienced that what happens to one seems to manifest in the other as well. One is dominant in the upward moving prāṇa, and the other in the downward moving apāna. Together, they make a whole, with each making up for what the other lacks and complimenting each other. Their fate is intertwined, regardless of the physical proximity or distance between the two.

Perhaps this has something to do with the theory of quantum teleportation - a phenomenon in which a quantum state is transferred between two particles via an intermediate particle that's entangled with them both. At the time of marriage, when fire enters the picture, there is the added entanglement of the husband and wife with that fire into which mantra-s are chanted during a marriage ritual. Thus, there is a bond, an entanglement created between the husband, wife and agni.

Quantum communications use photons to transmit qubits (a basic unit of quantum information) between remote places. When offerings are made to the fire to various deities or pitṛ-s, what is happening is a quantum communication to another dimension. For

---

132 Excerpt from the talks of Swami Vivekananda on 'The Women of India', delivered at Cambridge, Dec 17, 1894 and recorded in the book 'The complete works of Swami Vivekananda' by Advaitha Ashrama.

such a communication to be effective, the parties involved will have to be in quantum entangled states with each other.

However, with modern research in this field being really recent and largely looking at technological applications, it will be a while before we can apply the quantum understanding of photons to explain what is given in the śāstra-s, using the language of modern science. Until then, it might be better to take it for granted that the ancient ṛṣi-s knew what they were talking about and that modern science is just about beginning to touch the tip of that knowledge for material purposes.

Therefore, let us take it seriously when Jaimini (VI.1.17) establishes that husband and wife have to perform sacrifices together and not separately, and Āpastamba Dharma Sūtra (II.6.13.16-17) emphatically says that there can be no separation between husband and wife, for since marriage they have to perform religious acts jointly.[133]

Role of the wife

According to the śāstra-s, the first duty of the husband and the privilege of the wife was to require and to give her cooperation in all religious acts. In ṚgVeda (I.72.5)[134] it is said, 'they accompanied by their wives, worshipped the fire who is worthy of worship.' In another place, it is said, 'When you make the husband and wife of one mind, they anoint thee with ghee like a well-placed friend.' In the Taittirīya brāhmaṇa (III.7.5) is a passage: 'May the wife unite with her husband by means of good deeds (done by both), the two became yoked like oxen to the sacrifice.'[135]

---

133 जायापत्योर्न विभागो विद्यते । पाणिग्रहणादि सहत्वं कर्मसु । आप. ध. सू. II, 6, 13. 16-17.

134 संजानाना उप सीदन्नभिज्नु पत्नीवन्तो नमस्यं नमस्यन् । ऋ. I. 72. 5;

135 स पत्नी पत्या सुकृतेन गच्छताम् । यज्ञस्य युक्तौ धुर्यावभूताम् । संजानाना विजहतामरातीः । दिवि ज्योतिरजरमारभेताम् । तै. ब्रा. III. 7.5. Vide Dr. P.V. Kane 'History of Dharmasastra' Volume 2, Chapter XI – Rights and Duties on Marriage'

For a generation used to understanding things only when they manifest in obvious perceptible ways, it will be difficult to understand why a man has to be married to a woman for the sake of performing fire rituals when his wife seems to have no major role to play in terms of chanting or offering oblations to the fire. During aupāsana, for example, she has to only give her permission to the husband for him to proceed. But this silent presence and cooperation of the wife by giving permission is considered a must, without which a man is not eligible to perform the fire rituals.

So much so that some smṛti-s[136] mention that if a man's wife dies before him, he can create an effigy of his wife using kuśa grass or gold (as Śrī Rāma did for Sitā),[137] and only then will the agnihotra bear effect. Indeed, for this reason alone, men were encouraged to marry again if their wives died before them. Even a temporary absence of the wife was said to reduce the result of the sacrifice. For example, in Taittirīya brāhmaṇa (III.7.1), it says that half of the sacrifice is destroyed in the case of that sacrificer whose wife is (in her monthly course and, therefore) unavailable on the sacrificial day.[138]

Why is this importance attached to the wife? What, after all, is her role in a fire ritual?

The Veda-s declare 'यत् पिण्डे तत् ब्रह्माण्डे', meaning what is there in the microcosm is also there in the macrocosm. The subtle

---

136 Gobhila smṛti (III 9-10) - मृतायामपि भार्यायां वैदिकाग्निं न हि त्यजेत् । उपाधिनापि तत्कर्म यावज्जीवं सभा- पयेत् । रामोऽपि कृत्वा सौवर्णीं सीतां पत्नीं यशस्विनीम् । ईजे यज्ञैर्बहुविधैः सह भ्रातृभिरचिन्तैः ॥ गोभिलस्मृति III 9-10

137 काञ्चनीं मम पत्नीं च ' in रामायण VII. 91. 25.

138 Taittirīya brāhmaṇa (III.7.1) अर्धो वा एतस्य यज्ञस्य मीयते यस्य व्रत्येऽहन् पत्न्यनालम्भुका भवति । तामपरुध्य यजेत । सर्वेणैव यज्ञेन यजते ॥ तै.बा. III.7.1 'Indeed, half of this sacrifice is destroyed in the case of him whose wife becomes untouchable on the day on which the observances for a sacrifice commence (i.e. on the day previous to the performance); but the sacrificer should segregate her (in a different place) and offer the sacrifice; by doing so he worships with a sacrifice that is entire (though the wife is absent).' Vide History of Dharmaśāstra Vol 2, Part 2, Ch. XXII, Page 803.

movements of prāṇa within the microcosm of the human body can be understood by understanding the movement of prāṇa in the macrocosm. We can understand this by comparing prāṇa to electricity. The laws that apply to electricity are universal laws that also apply to the flow of prāṇa. After all, it is prāṇa that supports the flow of current.

When the husband, wearing the yajñopavīta (that is, the sacred thread on the left shoulder), chants Vedic mantra-s for the fire ritual, the sound vibrations cause the movement of electrons, and there is a build-up of current along the yajñopavīta, and a resulting magnetic field is created on the left side of his body (applying Fleming's Right Hand Rule). So far, current has been generated in the body but not yet directed towards the fire.

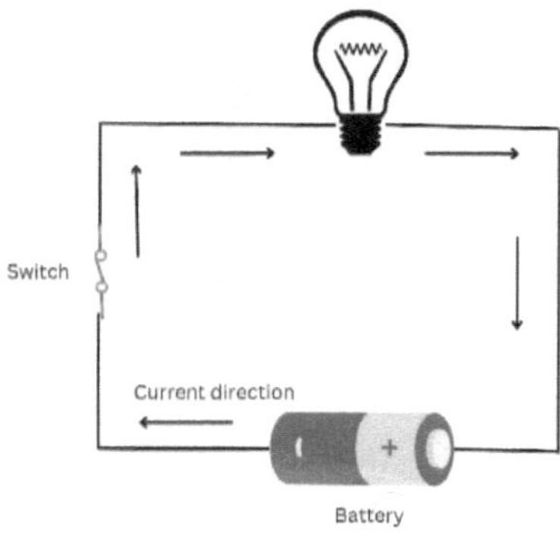

In any electrical circuit, for the built-up current (randomly moving electrons) to be made to flow in the circuit in a particular direction, there is a need for what is called *voltage*. Voltage is also called 'potential difference' because it results from a difference in potential between two points. For example, in a standard alkaline battery, we have two ends labelled + and -, which create a potential difference (voltage) causing current to flow in a circuit. Electrons are always released from the negative terminal of a battery and tend to go around a circuit to come back to the positive end of the battery. Anything placed in such a circuit (ex., a lightbulb) lights up because of the flow of the electrons from the negative to the positive end of the circuit.

In the human scenario of a fire ritual, the human male has built up electrons on his left side, owing to the sacred thread worn on the left. The male is only the negative terminal of a battery. To create a potential difference large enough to make the electrons move, thereby forming a circuit with the fire, there is a need for another entity which is similar in vibration to the male but of a lower current-carrying capacity. This is the role of the wife (ideally of the same varṇa), who, sitting to the right side of the husband, becomes the positive terminal of the battery. Husband and wife together create a potential difference (voltage), which is sufficient to move the electrons to the fire and back to the positive end of the battery (the right side of the wife).

Look at the brilliance of the design. If the wife were to be seated to the left side of the husband, forming the negative terminal of the battery, there would be hardly any current because she is not to chant mantra-s. Moreover, what the husband chanted would be received by the wife directly, and her body might not be able to take the high vibrations of such chants meant for agni. Further, if the wife were absent (and a suitable effigy not in place), then although the current is generated by the male, its movement would be very low because the inherent voltage of the man would not provide sufficient impetus to move the electrons in the circuit.

In any electrical circuit, all the devices and the connecting wire have a property known as resistance. As per Ohm's law, resistance (R) is inversely proportional to voltage (V). Therefore, only if the resistance is low can the voltage be high, causing easy movement of electrons in the circuit. In the human case, the mind is what offers resistance through the ego. When the husband surrenders his mind in bhakti to the divine, his resistance to make offerings to agni is lowered. Similarly, when the wife surrenders her ego in bhakti towards her husband, her resistance is lowered, and the two act as one in moving the current in the circuit.

Thus, we make sense of the śāstra injunctions, which say that the two (husband and wife) become one and act as one in a fire sacrifice, and without the wife's cooperation and presence, the results of the sacrifice are reduced by half. With this understanding, if we revisit the rules pertaining to fire rituals in chapter two, we will find a new meaning in them.

Transfer of charge

Since we are on the topic of current and charge (electrons), it is now possible to set right one of the most misunderstood concepts under varṇa dharma — the rules regarding touch. The human body is an efficient conductor and carries charge just as any other conductor. Based on one's varṇa and sādhanā practices, the amount of charge carried by individuals will differ. In physics, it is given that transfer of charge happens through friction (rubbing of a charged body against another), through conduction (by touching a charged body) and through induction (coming near to, but not touching, a charged body). Typically, when a body having more negative charge (more electrons) comes in contact with a body having more positive charge (or lesser electrons), the electrons move from the negatively charged body to the positively charged body. In other words, the current always moves from a point of high potential to low potential. This is how an individual's touch can cause a transfer of charge to the things or persons they touch.

Regardless of how electrons are transferred (through friction, conduction or induction), the total charge always remains the same. Electrons move, but they are not destroyed. This is the law of conservation of charge. Therefore, when two charged bodies touch each other, the charges flow between the bodies until the bodies have equal potential, i.e., the potentials of the two bodies become equal. So, a person having a higher charge will experience a reduced charge, and the person having a lower charge will gain a higher charge after coming near each other or by touching each other. Indeed, this is the reason for the rules of who and what to touch or not to touch, prescribed in the śāstra-s. These rules are given to people of every varṇa (including the śūdra) in case they come in contact with a person, animal or even an object that could lower their vibration. The prescriptions of taking a bath, sprinkling water, etc., if this happens, are meant to restore the lost charge since water is capable of supplying free electrons.

If these were meant as rules of caste-based impurity or untouchability as the accusation has been made, then the śāstra-s would not say that a person cannot touch his own son (whose thread ceremony has been performed) at the time of taking meals.[139] Similarly, the śāstra-s (Atri verse 249) specifically mentions that this rule of not touching does not apply in a temple, in religious processions, in marriages, in sacrifices and in all festivals. Just as a modern-day student of physics would easily understand the concept of charge transfer between objects, the ṛṣi-s understood the same at a human level and made rules accordingly, with the intention that people of every varṇa should be able to maintain the vibration that is conducive for them.

Note that, as mentioned earlier, the rules of varṇa dharma apply to those who identify with the physical body. Therefore, the rules of touch do not apply to those who have gone beyond body-identity, such as in the case of Guru-s.

Whenever modern scientists discovered a new law of the universe, they promptly used it to create applications for material well-being. In stark contrast, when the ancient masters, through their yogic siddhi, realised these universal laws, they found ways to apply them in day-to-day life for the purpose of every individual's health and spiritual well-being. Therefore, it is quite difficult to find existing research papers for spiritual practices and, similarly, to find direct evidence of technological advances of today in ancient scriptures. A minor attempt to accomplish this difficult task has been presented in this chapter, with the intention of pointing the direction in which we need to look to find answers that might satisfy the present generation.

---

139 Vide 'History of Dharmasastra' Part I, Vol II, Ch. IV. Page 170.

Chapter 7: Exceptions

We have all heard of varṇa 'by birth.' But according to the śāstra-s, each birth is only a continuation of the previous birth. More precisely, physical birth is the event that occurs after physical death in a previous birth. So, if varṇa is said to be based on birth, it actually means that it is based on death.

The thoughts, emotions and tendencies that one carries at the time of death in say, lifetime A, carry forward as one's varṇa in the next birth, say, lifetime B. This is regardless of what the person's varṇa by birth might have been in lifetime A. This is the crux of the matter in deciphering how each individual gets their inherent varṇa in each birth. To understand this better, we need to first understand what happens after death.

What happens at the time of death?

According to the Upaniṣad-s and Purāṇa-s, the human body is made up of the sthūla śarīra (physical body), sūkṣma śarīra (subtle body) and kāraṇa śarīra (causal body). When prāṇa leaves the human body completely, we call it physical death. When the body is cremated, the sthūla śarīra is reduced to ash. The sūkṣma śarīra also disperses with the help of the rituals performed and after experiencing its entitled fruits in various sūkṣma loka-s (subtle worlds). What remains intact birth after birth and re-attaches itself to the newborn in each birth is the kāraṇa śarīra.

In the Bhagvad Gītā, when Arjuna expresses doubt about all the good karma being futile in the next birth, Bhagavān Śrī Kṛṣṇa assures him that nothing is ever lost. All karma, good and bad, are recorded, stored and carried on birth after birth. This happens through the kāraṇa śarīra, which stores karma in the form of subtle vibrations.

While the karma stored in the kāraṇa śarīra as vibration is the sum total of all the actions performed by the jīva during its lifetime in human form, there is special importance attached to what happens at the moment of death. This is because the vibrations of thought that one carries at the moment of death determine where the ātma will take birth again since the ātma will be automatically attracted to a womb of similar vibration to continue its journey. It is like pausing a movie mid-way, and then when re-started, it automatically starts from the exact moment where it was paused. Once physical death takes place, the ātma cannot change its vibration; all it can do is find a womb with a matching vibration to take human birth again and complete its unfinished karma. Thus, thoughts held at the time of death determine the next birth vibrationally.

This is clearly stated by Śrī Kṛṣṇa in the below verse (Bhagavad Gītā 8.6), that whatever thoughts prominently dominate a person's mind at the moment of death determine his or her next birth.

यं यं वापि स्मरन्भावं त्यजत्यन्ते कलेवरम् |

तं तमेवैति कौन्तेय सदा तद्भावभावितः || 6||

'Whatever one remembers upon giving up the body at the time of death, O son of Kunti, one attains that state, being always absorbed in such contemplation.'

As per śāstra-s, it is our duty to ensure that a dying person listens to the name of Bhagavān repeatedly, thinks positively and leaves the body without attachments, fear or other negative emotions. Relatives of the dying person are often advised to offer dāna (charity) in the name of the dying person so that the vibration of the good karma performed in the name of the dying person attaches to the ātma after death. Instead, if the dying person carries negative emotions of fear, hatred, anger, etc., then regardless of the assigned varṇa in the present birth, the next birth will be of a vibrationally lower varṇa that matches the emotion felt at the time of death. In such cases, people will be born with saṃskāra-s (tendencies) of their earlier varṇa, but have the physical body of the present varṇa, which could sometimes be vibrationally lower than that of the saṃskāra they carry. For example, a śūdra who has the saṃskāra-s of a brāhmaṇa. This is what has happened in kali yuga, causing so much confusion regarding varṇa.

This understanding is necessary because it underlies the principle behind who we see as exceptions — they may be born as a woman, a śūdra or even a non-Hindu in this birth, but if they exhibit saṃskāra-s of another varṇa or the quality of enlightenment, it is certainly a result of karma accumulated in their previous births. This is what Hindu-s refer to as pūrva janma saṃskāra.

Siddhi-s

Often, people associate an enlightened being with the acquiring of siddhi-s (spiritual powers). Most exceptions that draw attention, such as Anasūyā, Dharmavyādha, Lopāmudra, etc., are due to their siddhi-s. So when we cite such exceptions to justify breaking the rules given in the śāstra-s, instead of enquiring how they might have attained their siddhi, we jump to conclusions assuming that they must have studied the Veda-s, chanted Vedic mantra-s and performed the karma of a brāhmaṇa and thus attained enlightenment.

An enlightened master once told me that siddhi-s are just the starting point of the spiritual journey, and it is not necessarily the quality of an enlightened being. It happens to many seekers at different phases in the spiritual journey and might not even last long. I was told that siddhi-s are the kindergarten of the spiritual journey and that anyone who does certain practices can acquire siddhi-s.

For example, the Śiva Saṃhita states that the siddhi pertaining to the mūlādhāra cakra can give one the ability to know the past, present and future. In kali yuga, the method used by some to achieve this is through the practice of specific techniques, mantras, etc., as given in tantra. But if such siddhi-s are acquired without overcoming the negative emotions of the said cakra, then it will backfire at some point. This is the reason why we see some practitioners of tantra who have siddhi-s but continue to display kāma, krodha, etc. and are after name, fame and material pursuits. They are not only dangerous to society, but also their siddhi-s will backfire at some point in their own life, creating unpleasant karma.

Examples of exceptions

In contrast, the stories of exceptions in the purāṇa-s show how the same can be acquired by performing one's varṇa dharma with sincerity and by surrendering one's aham through seva and bhakti. This should indeed be possible, given that each cakra is associated with a set of emotions. This means that by perfecting the positive emotions and letting go of the negative emotions, the cakra is activated, and its associated siddhi-s will manifest just by virtue of the right thought vibrations.

Most of the examples of exceptions given below are the stories which were narrated to me by enlightened masters in response to my specific questions about different aspects of varṇa dharma.

Anasūyā

An interesting story, especially for women, is that of Anasūyā. This story is given in Śrī Guru Caritra. I received this story when I enquired how women could protect themselves since they have no adhikāra for Gāyatrī and other mantra-s which build an aura of high vibration and thus protect men.

Asūyā means jealousy, and Anasūyā means one who knows no jealousy. Anasūyā was the wife of ṛṣi Atri and a woman who was chaste and pure, adhering to all the rules of pativratā dharma. The story goes that she was so pure that the Trimūrti-s, Brahma, Viṣṇu and Śiva decided to test her chastity. One day, the Trimūrti-s, in the form of three mendicants, knocked on her door for alms when her husband was away. As was the norm, she gently invited them to her house and offered them food. However, the mendicants told her that they would only accept food from her if she gave it to them while being unclothed. Anasūyā then used her siddhi-s acquired through her inner purity and transformed the three mendicants into three infants. She then produced breast milk at will and fed them with her breast milk, which was also another siddhi. When her husband, ṛṣi Atri, came home, he understood what had happened and who the infants were. The infants were then transformed into their original forms as the Trimūrti-s, who then blessed the couple. Upon the request of Anasūyā that they be born through her, she had three sons, one of whom was the great Guru Śrī Dattatreya. Śri Dattatreya is thus said to be the incarnation of the Trimūrti-s.

How could pativratā dharma give Anasūyā such siddhi-s?

Regarding the siddhi-s obtained through pativratā dharma, much has been mentioned in the purāṇa-s. For example, the Skanda Purāṇa[140] names several pativratā-s like Arundhatī, Anasūyā,

---

140 Skanda Purāṇa III, Brahma Khaṇḍa, Brahmāraṇya section Chapter 7. The mention of names is in verses 14-15. Vide Dr. P.V. Kane's 'History of Dharmaśāstra Volume II, Part 1.

Sāvitrī, Śāṇḍilyā, Satyā, Menā and then talks about the tremendous spiritual power of a pativratā, saying 'just as a snake-charmer forcibly draws out from a hole a snake, so a pativratā snatches away her husband's life from the messengers of death and reaches heaven with her husband. And the messengers of death, on seeing a pativrata, beat a hasty retreat.' The Śalyaparva (63) narrates how awful the power of a pativratā like Gandhari is in that she can, if she chooses, burn the world, and she can even stop the motions of the sun and the moon.

Let us try to understand why such power was attributed to a pativratā.

There are three subtle sources of vibration — light, sound and thought. Just as the dvija-s use light and sound vibrations to purify their karma, non-dvija-s and women have been shown the path of using thought vibrations. One such path is pativratā dharma, which prescribes chastity in thought and actions as its core practice. When chastity is thus ingrained in a woman, the kāma (desire and lust) vibrations of low frequency melt away. Kāma, which results in attachment, is the cause of all the other negative vibrations that follow, such as krodha (anger), lobha (greed), moha (delusion), madā (arrogance) and mātsarya (jealousy) — all of which are traits associated with the svādhiṣṭhāna cakra (connected to reproductive organs). So, for a woman, controlling kāma through chastity is considered to give equal merit as that acquired by men who control kāma through the practice of brahmacārya.

The other requirement of pativratā dharma, as per the śāstra-s is that women see their husbands as Bhagavān, even if the husband is full of flaws, impotent, devoid of limbs, of evil character, etc.[141] This

---

141 Refer Śatapatha Brāhmana (IV.1.5.9), Śankha Likhita II, part 1, Manu (V.154) and Yājñavalkya I.77. Vide Dr. P.V. Kane 'History of Dharmaśāstra Volume II, Part 1, Chapter XI.

difficult-to-grasp concept can be better understood through the story of Sant Nāmdev.

> Sant Nāmdev was such that he saw Bhagavān, his Panduranga Vittala, in everything and everyone. Once, Nāmdev stayed in a deserted house in a village. The villagers told him not to stay there, as that house was said to be haunted by a Brahma-Rākshas.[142] At midnight, the dreadful Brahma-Rākshas appeared before Nāmdev in a form that was very long and fear-inducing.
>
> For Nāmdev, however, the entire world was the abode of his Bhagavān, and Vittala alone existed in the form of all creatures, so much so that even the Brahma-Rākshas appeared to Nāmdev as Vittala. Nāmdev started singing the praise of Vittala, saying, "O my Bhagavān Vittala, You have appeared in the elongated form of a Brahma-Rākshas today. Your head is touching the heavens, and Your feet are on the earth. No one can describe this form of yours fully. You are my Lord, shower Your grace on me." Instantly, Nāmdev saw his Pandurang Vittala showing His glimpse with the conch, cakra, mace and lotus flower in His hands. Thus, even the Brahma-Rākshas was transformed just by virtue of Sant Nāmdev's ability to see Bhagavān in everyone.

You might agree that the śāstra-s are less demanding of women, given that we only need to see our human husband as divine! In a small experiment carried out by a friend who learned about this, the results were surprisingly positive, with the unsuspecting subject of her experiment becoming kinder and more considerate towards his wife without realising why. The only way to really know if this works is to test it yourself. At the very least, we need to understand and become aware that the way people behave with us is influenced by our own

---

142 It is said that when one who is of a Brāhmana varṇa commits dreadful sins such as insulting the Veda-s or committing suicide, he/she upon death becomes a Brahma-rākshas.

thought vibrations. The śāstra-s, too, meant this when they stated that it does not matter how many bad qualities a woman's husband has; she has to raise herself to see Bhagavān in him.

The deeper understanding is this. Just as an arcaka invokes a deity in a stone by virtue of the strength and purity of his saṅkalpa, transforming it into a living devatā, a pativratā woman too can transform her husband by the strength and purity of her ability to see the divine in him. In the process of doing this, the woman herself would attain spiritual powers. If we contemplate this, we realise that through pativratā dharma, the śāstra-s are guiding women to straightaway work towards that highest goal of spirituality, which is to see the divine in others. This is given in the words of Śrī Kṛṣṇa in Śrīmad Bhāgavatam (11.29.15):

नरेष्वभीक्ष्णं मद्भावं पुंसो भावयतोऽचिरात् । स्पर्धासूयातिरस्काराः साहङ्कारा वियन्ति हि ॥ १५॥

'Ideas of rivalry, jealousy, abusiveness and egotism quickly depart from a person who always thinks of Me in all men.'

Thus, every ordinary woman who, through the practice of pativratā dharma, cleanses her mind and becomes like Anasūyā can obtain the siddhi of making others become what she sees them to be.

The incident of Anasūyā being able to feed the infants is an indication of having cultivated the virtue of the heights of matrubhāv (motherhood). There are real-life stories, too, such as that of the Kashmiri female saint Lal Ded (also known as Lalleshwari),[143] who induced breast milk at will to feed a child in need. These instances are called emotionally induced pseudo-lactation (technically called galactorrhoea) by modern science. In a case study,[144] scientists tried

---

143 The Book of Lalla Ded Lalleshwari, by Paul Smith

144 Dissanayake H, Keerthisena S, Dematapitiya C, Katulanda P. Emotionally induced galactorrhoea in a non-lactating female--"Pseudo- Lactation"? BMC Endocr Disord. 2014 Dec 17;14:98. doi: 10.1186/1472-6823-14-98. PMID: 25518745; PMCID: PMC4289561.

to analyse why a non-pregnant young woman found herself lactating whenever she saw her neighbour's newborn infant, heard its cries or even had a memory of it. While scientists try to explain it in their own technical language, it is nothing short of a siddhi that comes from the heightened experience of motherhood.

This ability of ordinary women to transform into mothers by just transforming their emotions is their greatest protection. In the story of Anasūyā, we see how even the strange request of the mendicants to be fed unclothed could not shake her chastity and her matrubhāv. It will help women to be mindful of the fact that we only attract that which matches our own frequency of vibration. When women cultivate the ability to feel like a mother to all, their vibrations will be higher and of the anāhata (heart) cakra; this will automatically protect women from all negative intentions, which are low-frequency vibrations of the svādhiṣṭhāna and mūlādhāra cakra.

Dharmavyādha

Dharmavyādha's story was narrated by ṛṣi Mārkandeya to Yudhiṣṭhira, in the Mahābhārata Vanaparva (Section 204 onwards). I received this story when I enquired if a non-brāhmaṇa, especially women or śūdra-s, can have siddhi-s or become spiritually enlightened.

This is the story of a brāhmaṇa named Kaushika who was astounded to find that an ordinary but chaste woman (name not mentioned) and a butcher[145] (Dharmavyādha) by virtue of following their respective dharma had siddhi-s equal to that of the brāhmaṇa. In this story, we see that the butcher answers the brāhmaṇa's questions on subtle aspects of karma, birth and the afterlife, which is at par with what the upaniṣad-s reveal. The butcher also teaches the brāhmaṇa the rules of varṇa dharma given in the śāstra-s without having typically studied them since his varṇa would not have permitted him to study these texts. Surprised at his wisdom and

---

145 In some versions of this story, he is described as a fowler.

knowledge, the brāhmaṇa asks him about his previous birth and finds that the butcher was a learned brāhmaṇa in his previous birth and, due to a mistake, was cursed to be born as a butcher.

This story is so complete in itself that it explains almost everything that this book has been attempting to convey. A simplified and shorter version of the story is presented below.

A brāhmaṇa named Kaushika was a virtuous ascetic who had studied all the Veda-s with the anga-s and the upaniṣad-s. Once, while he was sitting under a tree reciting Veda-s, a female crane perched atop the tree defiled his head with droppings. Kaushika became very angry. Such was his siddhi that just by his thought of anger directed at the bird, the crane dropped dead. Seeing the dead crane, he was moved by pity and said to himself, "Alas, I have done a wrong deed overcome by anger and malice!" Having told himself this several times in repentance, he entered a village to beg for alms.

He stood in front of a house asking for alms. The lady of the house asked him to wait while she was engaged in cleaning the utensil from which alms were given. Suddenly, her husband arrived, afflicted with hunger. The chaste woman then attended to her husband, following all the rules of pativratā dharma, forgetting the brāhmaṇa waiting for alms.

When she remembered that she had kept the brāhmaṇa waiting, she felt abashed and immediately came out with alms for Kaushika and apologised to him for keeping him waiting. Kaushika chastised her for keeping a brāhmaṇa waiting and for considering her domestic duties more important than attending to a brāhmaṇa. Out of anger, he said to her, "Proud woman, don't you know that brāhmaṇa-s are like fire and may consume the entire earth?"

At these words, the woman answered, "I am no she-crane O ṛṣi! You, who is endued with the wealth of asceticism, cast off this anger of yours! Enraged as you are, what can you do to me with these angry glances of yours? I do not disregard Brāhmaṇa-s........but my heart is inclined to that merit which springs forth from the service of my husband, for I regard my husband as the highest among all gods. Behold, O ṛṣi, the merit that attaches to the service of one's husband. I know that you have burnt a female crane with your wrath. But, the anger that a person cherishes is the greatest of foes that the person has."

So saying, she described to him what the qualities of a brāhmaṇa should be. She finally tells him that although he may have studied the Veda-s, he seems to not know what the highest virtue is in reality. She then asks him to go and meet a virtuous butcher in the city of Mithila, who is devoted to the service of his parents and has his senses completely under control. She once again asked him to forgive her, and this time, the brāhmaṇa forgave and, reproaching himself for his anger, returned to his abode.

Kaushika's faith in the woman's words, assured by her knowledge of the death of the crane and the words of virtuous import that she had uttered, made him decide to go and meet the butcher in Mithila. When he reached Mithila and finally found the butcher, Kaushika saw him seated in a butcher's yard, selling meat. Due to the large crowd of buyers gathered around the butcher, Kaushika stood at a distance. But the butcher, apprehending that the brāhmaṇa had come to him, suddenly rose from his seat and went to that secluded spot where the brāhmaṇa was. He then saluted him and said, "Command me as to what I may do for you. The words that the chaste woman said to you are known to me. I also know for what purpose you have come here." Hearing these words, Kaushika thought, "This is the second marvel that I have seen. First, the lady who knew about the incident with the crane, and now, this butcher who knows what the lady had told me." The butcher then offers to take the brāhmaṇa to his house as it would be more appropriate, and Kaushika gladly agrees.

In the butcher's house, the brāhmaṇa Kaushika tells him that the current occupation of a butcher does not seem appropriate for him.

To this remark, the butcher replies, "O brāhmaṇa, this profession is that of my family, and I have inherited it from my sires and grandsires. Grieve not for my adhering to the duties that belong to me by birth. Discharging the duties ordained for me by the creator, with care, I serve my superiors and the aged. I always speak the truth, never envy others, and give to the best of my power. I live upon what remains after serving the gods, guests and those who depend on me. I never speak ill of anyone, small or great. O best of brāhmaṇa, the actions of a former life always follow the doer..." So saying, the butcher explains the duties prescribed for each varṇa.

Interestingly, the butcher also speaks about himself thus: "As regards me, O brāhmaṇa, I always sell meat without slaying the animals myself. I sell meat of animals that have been slain by others. I never eat meat myself; I never go to my wife except in her season; I always fast during the day and eat at night. Even though the behaviour of his order is bad, a person may yet be himself of good behaviour. So also a person may become virtuous although he may be a butcher by profession."

Impressed by his words, the brāhmaṇa questions the butcher about what is the highest virtue, how one acquires karma at birth, what are the senses and how to control them, what are the five elements and their qualities, the qualities of sattva, rajas, tamas, etc., all of which were eloquently explained by the butcher. The butcher also tells him about the dharma of a brāhmaṇa and why they are to be respected as a class.

And then, the butcher reveals the secret of how he knows all of this and the reason for his inner spiritual vision by introducing the brāhmaṇa to his aged parents. The butcher says to the brāhmaṇa, "They, my parents, are the devatā-s that I offer pūjā to. Whatever is due unto the gods, I do unto them. As the thirty-three gods with Indira as their head receive offerings of pūjā by all men, so do these aged parents of mine receive pūjā offerings from me. As brāhmaṇa-s exert themselves for the purpose of procuring offerings for their gods, so do I act with diligence for these two. They, my father and mother, are supreme gods, and I seek to please them always with offerings of flowers, fruits and gems. To me, they are like the sacred fire mentioned by the learned, and they seem to me to be as good as the four Veda-s…..by serving them properly, one acquires the merit of perpetually keeping up the sacred fire."

Completely in awe of the butcher, the brāhmaṇa told him, "As it is very difficult for a person of the śūdra varṇa to learn the mysteries of life, I do not consider you to be a śūdra. There must surely be some mystery in connection with this matter. You must have attained the state of a śūdra by reason of some past karma. Do tell me what it is."

And then the butcher says that indeed, in a previous birth, he was a brāhmaṇa, well read in the Veda-s and an accomplished student of the Vedanga-s, and through his own fault, he has been born as a śūdra. He then narrated that a king had taught him archery, and once, when they went hunting, the brāhmaṇa's arrow unknowingly pierced the body of a ṛṣi. The ṛṣi, out of anger, cursed him to be born in the next birth as a butcher in the śūdra varṇa. When the brāhmaṇa repeatedly expressed his regret and apologised to the ṛṣi, the ṛṣi said that he could not take back his curse but could bless him that even though he would be a śūdra in the next birth, he would remain a pious man who will honour his parents and through that, he would attain spiritual perfection and go to heaven. The ṛṣi also told him that he would remember his past life and that on expiation of this curse, he would again become a brāhmaṇa.

Through this story, we get the message that even though one has the saṃskāra-s and wisdom of a learned brāhmaṇa from a previous birth, he should only follow the dharma of his current birth. It also gives a hint that only in the birth as a brāhmaṇa can one acquire the deeper knowledge of dharmaśāstra-s. Such knowledge, once acquired, remains even if the subsequent birth is of a śūdra varṇa.

Viśvāmitra

Viśvāmitra was a king, a kṣatriya named Kaushika, who, through severe tapas, finally attained the status of a brahmarṣi, which is a title usually only given to a brāhmaṇa. I received this story when I enquired if a non-brāhmaṇa can vibrationally become a brāhmaṇa in the same birth, and if yes, what it takes for that to happen.

The story of King Kaushika (before being named Viśvāmitra) being desirous of owning the sacred cow which belonged to ṛṣi Vasiṣṭha is well known. Kaushika even wages a battle against ṛṣi Vasiṣṭha, but is easily defeated by the ṛṣi just by virtue of his yogic powers. That is when Kaushika decides to undertake severe tapas to become even more powerful than ṛṣi Vasiṣṭha. This ego-driven pursuit gave him many siddhi-s, but it was also evident that he kept losing his powers with the slightest temptation. The story of Menaka seducing him and his having a child with her is one such. His control over his senses is tested again when Rambha is sent by Indira to seduce him; this time, he loses his temper and curses her to become a stone. After each such incident of distraction, he would restart his tapas, lasting a few thousand years.

Finally, after several thousand years of tapas, he finally manages to control all his senses, and Śrī Brahma declares him a brahmarṣi and names him Viśvāmitra, meaning one who is a friend of all. At this point, it is said that Viśvāmitra wanted ṛṣi Vasiṣṭha to acknowledge him as a brahmarṣi, and so he went to ṛṣi Vasiṣṭha.

The enlightened Master who narrated this to me said that when Viśvāmitra looked at the radiant, peaceful face of ṛṣi Vasiṣṭha, who kept silent, Viśvāmitra realised that he was still lacking and a trace of ego still remained in him. He then just gave up and surrendered to ṛṣi Vasiṣṭha. In that moment of surrender, the great ṛṣi Vasiṣṭha said, "Now you have become a brahmarṣi."

What is of significance in this story is that through his sādhanā, though he acquired many siddhi-s, in the end, it took a burning of his physical body through severe tapas, control over all his senses, and complete surrender of his ego to be finally declared a brahmarṣi.

Guru-s in female form

It is a similar intense breaking of the physical body that we see in the case of Guru-s born with a female form. The biography of enlightened beings in female form, such as Shiva Yogini Amma,[146] Śrī Māta Amritānandamayī Devī,[147] Śrī Ānandamayi Ma,[148] and Akka Mahādevī[149] describes how they had to go through the fire of intense tapas that transformed their physical body in the process of attaining enlightenment. Needless to say, this is an agonisingly painful process for the body. Besides, all the Guru-s mentioned above attained oneness with the divine through intense bhakti and not by chanting the Veda-s. The knowledge of the Veda-s was revealed to them after they attained the enlightened state. Therefore, citing the case of enlightened beings in female form as proof that all women can study the Veda-s or chant Vedic mantra-s, etc., is misleading. Moreover, even after the efforts, being able to achieve the final goal is a result of pūrva janma saṃskāra and only one in a few million can even attain this status by such effort. The others will only damage their body and mind by forcefully taking the path of these exceptional cases.

Maitreyi

An example often quoted is that of Maitreyi, the wife of ṛṣi Yājñavalkya, who received the Brahma Vidyā from him just as he

146 The Master Mystic: The Life of Shiva Yogini Amma, book by Nitya Menon. 2007

147 Amma: The biography of Sri Mata Amritanandamayi Devi, by Swami Amritaswarupananda Puri. 1998

148 The Essential Sri Anandamayi Ma, biography by Alexander Lipski, 2007.

149 Sky Clad: The Extraordinary Life and Times of Akka Mahadevi, by Mukunda Rao. 2018

himself prepared to take sanyāsa. She was neither a brahmavādini nor a ṛṣika, yet she was considered eligible to receive this vidyā. It was her desire to learn the highest truth, rejecting all material wealth which he offered her, that earned her this right and not because she was proficient in the Veda-s, as is usually assumed.

Perhaps it should also be mentioned what is meant by Brahma Vidyā because some might assume that it is some important Vedic ritual. Brahma Vidyā is the teaching that gives one the realisation to connect with the ātma within as the source of Brahman, similar to what many of the upaniṣad-s teach. This is the path to reaching spiritual enlightenment through jñāna (and not karma). To be eligible for it, one has to completely give up worldly pursuits and surrender to the divine. It has nothing to do with reading Vedic texts, chanting Vedic mantra-s or performing Vedic rituals.

Bhagavān Śrī Kṛṣṇa explicitly makes it known to Uddhava as to who is eligible for this highest knowledge of Brahma Vidyā (also known as ātma vidyā), in the following verses of Śrīmad Bhāgavatam (11.29.30),

नैतत्त्वया दाम्भिकाय नास्तिकाय शठाय च ।

अशुश्रूषोरभक्ताय दुर्विनीताय दीयताम् ॥ ३० ॥

'You should not share this instruction with anyone who is hypocritical, atheistic or dishonest, or with anyone who will not listen faithfully, who is not a devotee, or who is simply not humble.'

एतैर्दोषैर्विहीनाय ब्रह्मण्याय प्रियाय च ।

साधवे शुचये ब्रूयाद् भक्तिः स्याच्छूद्रयोषिताम् ॥ ३१ ॥

'This knowledge should be taught to one who is free from these bad qualities, who is devoted to brāhmaṇa-s, and who is kindly disposed, saintly and pure, aye, even to the śūdra-s and women, should they have devotion.'

These were the qualities that made Maitreyi eligible to receive the Brahma Vidyā, and as said by Bhagavān, even the śūdra varṇa and women can receive it if they have the above-mentioned qualities.

Gārgi

In a bit of a contrast, the other lady mentioned in connection with ṛṣi Yājñavalkya, by the name Gārgi, who is known to have asked him questions in the court of King Janaka, was silenced by the ṛṣi for her somewhat thoughtless questioning. This conversation is shared below.

> "Then Gārgi, the daughter of Vacaknu, asked him. Yājñavalkya, she said, 'If all this is pervaded by water, by what is water pervaded?' 'By air, O Gārgi.' 'By what is air pervaded?' 'By the sky, O Gārgi.' 'By what is the sky pervaded?' 'By the world of the Gandharvas, O Gārgi.' 'By what is the world of the Gandharvas pervaded?' 'By the sun, O Gārgi.' 'By what is the sun pervaded?' 'By the moon, O Gārgi.' 'By what is the moon pervaded?' 'By the stars, O Gārgi.' 'By what are the stars pervaded?' 'By the world of the gods, O Gārgi.' 'By what is the world of the gods pervaded?' 'By the world of Indra, O Gārgi.' 'By what is the world of Indra pervaded?' 'By the world of Virāj, O Gārgi.' 'By what is the world of Viraj pervaded?' 'By the world of Hiranyagarbha, O Gārgi.' 'By what is the world of Hiranyagarbha pervaded?' He said, 'Do not, O Gārgi, push your inquiry too far, lest your head should fall off. You are questioning a deity that should not be reasoned about. Do not, O Gārgi, push your inquiry too far.' Thereupon, Gārgi, the daughter of Vacaknu, kept silent."[150]

---

150 Bṛhadāranyaka Upanishad Chapter 3, Section VI, Verse 1 – Last sentence by Yājñavalkya: स होवाच, गार्गि मातिप्राक्षीः, मा ते मूर्धा व्यपप्तत् अनतिप्रश्न्यां वै देवतामतिपृच्छसि गार्गि, मातिप्रक्षीरिति; ततो ह गार्गी वाचक्कयुपरराम ॥ १

Often, enthusiastic Vedic activists club Gārgi and Maitreyi together, sometimes as brahmavādini-s and sometimes as ṛṣikā-s, intending to provide evidence that women were taught Vedic mantra-s. However, there is a lot of finer understanding that will reveal why this is a wrong assumption to make because neither was shown as proficient in Vedic mantra chanting nor as performing karma kānda rituals. Yes, Gārgi is referred to as a brahmavādini, but not a ṛṣika because she was not a seer of mantra-s. The path of a brahmavādini was more of the jñāna mārg and not the karma marg. Therefore, citing them to justify teaching girls Vedic mantra-s is quite incorrect.

Ṛṣika-s

The ṛṣika-s mentioned in the Veda-s are the ones to whom some of the sūkta-s (hymns), especially of the ṚgVeda, have been attributed. They attained the status of a ṛṣika because they are said to have been the dṛṣta (seer) of the sūkta. Such an ability is certainly a siddhi and such siddhi-s are possible only through the blessings of enlightened ṛṣi-s. Therefore, it is not a coincidence that almost all the ṛṣika-s had as their Guru, husbands, or fathers who were ṛṣi-s. In other cases, they were celestial beings themselves (e.g., Urvaśī, the apsara) or were the consort of a devatā. A few details are given below of the nature of the sūkta-s composed by well-known ṛṣika-s, taken from the book 'Ṛṣika-s of the ṚgVeda.'[151]

Ghoṣā, daughter of ṛṣi Kakṣivān, had a terrible disease and was unmarried until the age of sixty. She fell into grief thinking about her age, about still being unmarried and not having a son. She prayed to the Aśvins to free her from disease and to bless her with beauty and good fortune. Thus, she is said to have seen the two mantra-s composed in praise of the Aśvins, who are said to have cured her of

---

151 Reference and source is taken from the book 'Ṛṣika-s of the ṚgVeda' by Swamini Atmaprajnananda Saraswati. 2013

her disease, made her ageless, beautiful and gave her a husband. She also had a son who became sage Suhastya. Her compositions can be read in ṚgVeda X.39, containing fourteen mantra-s, eulogising the Aśvins and X.40, containing fourteen mantra-s expressing her personal and intimate feelings and desires of a married life.

Lopāmudrā, the wife of ṛṣi Agastya, is the seer of the first two ṛcā of ṚgVeda 1.179, containing six ṛcā. Of these, the initial four are addressed to Rati and are an intimate conversation between her and ṛṣi Agastya. She served her husband faithfully for many years but felt a lack of marital bliss due to his practice of celibacy. These compositions convey this message to her husband, seeking his love and attention.

Apālā Atreyi, the daughter of ṛṣi Atri, composed a prayer to Indira, as she was forsaken by her husband after contacting a cutaneous disease. In one of the lines of her compositions, she asks Indira for three boons - to make three regions sprout, that is, her father's head, the cornfield, and the region below her belly. She is the seer of the whole sūkta ṚgVeda VIII.91.

Indrāni, the consort of Indra, is the seer of the ṚgVeda X.145, which is a spell to rid a jealous wife of a more favoured rival. The last mantra in this is intended to win the love of her husband, while the rest of the five are meant to get rid of a rival co-wife.

Similar is the case of Śacī Paulomi, who is considered the wife of Indira. She is the seer of ṚgVeda X.159, which is a song of triumph by Śacī over her rival co-wives.

Among the lesser-known names are Urvaśī, the apsara who is credited with ṚgVeda X.95, which is a conversation between her and King Purūravā after she leaves him, and he tries to convince his lady-love to return to him. Then there is Yamī Vaivasvatī, the twin sister of Yama, who is credited with some mantra-s in ṚgVeda 10 known as Yama-Yamī- Saṃvāda, in which she entreats her brother Yama to become her husband as there is no one else to perpetuate the human race. Yama refuses and eventually dies. ṚgVeda X.154 is a Funeral Hymn, which is also attributed to Yamī. There is also Śāśvatī Āṅgirasī, daughter of ṛṣi Āṅgiras, who is the seer of ṚgVeda VIII.1.34, which is dedicated to her husband after her husband got back his lost virility and pleased her.

The mantra-s attributed to ṛṣika-s that are uttered even today are the Devī Sūktam by Vāgāmbhṛṇi, Rātri Sūktam by Rātri Bhāradvājī, both of which are part of Durgāsaptaśatī Caṇḍī, and also the Sūryā-Sāvitrī-Sūktam which is credited to Sūryā-Sāvitrī, the daughter of Sūrya and is uttered during marriage rituals.

Thus, we see that among the sūkta-s attributed to 27 ṛṣika-s,[152] most of the sūkta-s have something to do with the ṛṣika's relationship with her husband/consort, sexuality, being rid of disease or a rival co-wife, and requests for good health. In a few cases, the sūkta-s are in praise of a deity such as Agni, Indira or the Aśvins (not shared here). Still fewer are the ones where the ṛṣika fully identified herself with the deity, and she herself is the devatā composing hymns such as the Devi Sūktam, etc.

Most of these mantra-s, by their nature, correlate to the lower cakra-s and are intended to provide health, well-being, marital bliss and fulfilment of desires in general. Isn't it an irony that in the name of these ṛṣika-s, young girls today are being taught the Gāyatri mantra, Mahāmṛtyuñjaya mantra (tryambakaṃ yajāmahe of the ṚgVeda VII.59.12), Śrī Rudram, etc. which correspond to the higher cakra-s and are not meant for the female body? Moreover, hardly do we hear of the mantra-s of the well-known ṛṣika-s mentioned above being taught to girls. It is indeed worth contemplating why this is so.

---

152 Reference and Source is taken from the book 'Ṛṣika-s of the ṚgVeda' by Swamini Atmaprajnananda Saraswati. 2013

Yoga and Yoginī

With the popularity of esoteric yogic techniques now being taught to women, it is essential to know why these were not encouraged for women in the past. And even now, what would it take for a woman's body to accomplish the final goal of specialised yogic techniques?

One who accomplishes the final goal of yoga is called a yogī (if male) or a yoginī (if female). The final goal of yoga is to surrender one's individual identity and establish oneself in the divine. Yoga, in that sense, simply means union. Union of what?

In the practice of yoga through traditions such as that of Hatha Yoga, 'yogic union' refers to the union of the śakti tattva with the śiva tattva. Here, śakti is referred to as the kuṇḍalini that lies coiled at the base of the spine in the mūlādhāra cakra, and śiva is referred to as that which is seated at the crown of one's head in the sahasrāra cakra. Therefore, the yogic techniques aim to achieve the union of śakti with śiva by forcing the kuṇḍalini situated in the mūlādhāra to uncoil and rise up the subtle suṣumṇa nādi inside the spinal column, piercing each of the six cakra-s on its way up, until it reaches the sahasrāra cakra.

This is done by making the practitioner perform various types of bandha-s and breathing techniques, which forcibly turn prāṇa upwards. When prāṇa thus turns upwards, all the lower bodily functions managed by the downward moving prāṇa (also called apāna) begin to get impacted. Digestion, excretion and sexual functions, therefore, get affected. This is mentioned in the Haṭhapradīpikā[153] text as given below:

अधोगतमपानं वै ऊर्ध्वगं कुरुते हठात् ॥

आकुञ्चनेन तं प्राहुर्मूलबन्धं तु योगिनः ॥ 80 ॥

'The apāna is raised upwards with force by contracting (the anus). Yogī-s call this mūla-bandha.' - 80

---

153 Haṭhapradīpikā of Svātmārāma, Chapter 5, verses 80 - 83

अपानप्राणयोरैक्यात् क्षयान् मूत्रपुरीषयोः ||

युवा भवति वृद्धोऽपि सततं मूलबन्धनात् || 83 ||

'Through consistent practice of mūla-bandha, prāṇa and apāna are united, reducing faeces and urine and as a result, an old (person) becomes young.' - 83

To facilitate this upward movement of apāna and to achieve the final goal of yoga, those practising Hatha Yoga are asked to maintain celibacy, eat specific food that is easy to digest, stay in seclusion, etc.[154]

When it comes to women of menstrual age, if they practice bandha-s and force apāna upwards, it will obviously impact menstruation. The downward flow of menstruation is facilitated by the downward moving force of apāna. So when apāna itself is forced upwards, there will be difficulty menstruating. Prolonged inversion of apāna could also result in painful conditions such as endometriosis, in which the menstrual blood itself turns upwards by the force of the upward moving apāna.

Another aspect of Hatha Yoga is to conserve the human seed and turn it upwards, transforming it into subtler forms. For men, this is achieved through the practice of celibacy, which retains the semen, and then they use certain techniques which turn it upwards. As discussed before, men have within their body both the X and Y chromosomes (in gross form), representing the śakti and śiva elements, respectively (in subtle form), so they can attempt such techniques for achieving the yogic union.

Whereas, for women, the seed, which is the egg, is voluntarily released every month during menstruation. Moreover, without the Y chromosome, how can they achieve the yogic union?

---

154 Verses 42 to 58 of Chapter 1 of Haṭhapradīpikā of Svātmārāma mention the rules to be followed for a practitioner of Hatha Yoga

Whether modern teachers of Hatha Yoga realise this or not, they insist that women too can practice this form of yoga and become yoginī-s. Technically, they are, of course, not wrong, but do they and the women practitioners of Hatha Yoga fully understand what it takes to accomplish the feat of becoming a yoginī?

Haṭhapradīpikā Chapter 5 states,

ऋतुमत्या रजोऽप्येव निज बिन्दुं च रक्षयेत् ॥

मेढ्रे णाकर्षयेदूर्ध्व सम्यगभ्यासयोगवान् ॥ 129 ॥

'A menstruating woman should preserve the rajas, a man should preserve his bindu, by raising it upwards by contracting the perineum through the appropriate practice.' - 29

पुंसो बिन्दुं समाकुञ्च्य सम्यगभ्यासपाटवात् ॥

यदि नारी रजो रक्षेत् संयोगे चापि योगिनी ॥ 135 ॥।

'A woman is considered a yoginī who, through appropriate practice, draws bindu of a man and unites it with rajas.' - 135

तस्याः किञ्चिद्रजो नाशं न गच्छति न संशयः ॥

तस्याः शरीरे नादस्तु बिन्दुतामेव गच्छति ॥ 136 ॥

'Undoubtedly, she (such a yoginī) will not waste even a droplet of rajas. In her body, the nāda will get transformed into bindu (light).' - 136

Let us understand what the above verses mean. 'Bindu' refers to the male seed contained in semen. 'Rajas' refers to menstrual blood. The technique prescribed here for a woman practitioner of Hatha Yoga is to draw in the semen and unite it with menstrual blood, turning both upwards.

Are women practitioners of Hatha Yoga aware that the entire practice is intended to stop them from menstruating? Are they also aware that even such stoppage of menstruation will not result in the final goal of becoming a yoginī unless they receive the male semen and undertake the prescribed technique?

Needless to say, the ultimate goal of Hatha Yoga for women — to become a yoginī — will result in menstrual disorders or pregnancy if done without proper guidance. It might have occurred to readers that this same outcome is also possible, in a safer way, through vivāha and pativratā dharma given in the dharmaśāstra texts.

This does not mean that women should not practice simpler versions of yogāsana-s or prāṇāyāma. In the absence of the traditional means of exercise through household work, which was apt for a woman's body, yoga has become the next best alternative. But women should take care not to practice anything that causes inversion of apāna, such as bandha-s, śirśasana (inverted headstand) and also avoid any pose that puts stress on the uterus, such as mayūrāsana. Even the practice of dhyāna (meditation) for women of menstrual age is better if done focusing on the heart (anāhata cakra) rather than the space between the eyebrows (ājña cakra). Also, neither āsana nor prāṇāyāma nor dhyāna should be practised during menstruation, as it will impact the downward moving apāna, which is naturally active during menstruation.

There is an increasing trend of yoga teachers recommending 'yoga for period pain.' The truth is that if yoga was done right during non-menstruating times, there would be no need for yoga during menstruation. Poses that cause inversion of apāna are the reason for period pain among yoga practitioners. Countering these with some more āsana-s during menstruation is like causing fire and then making a business out of fire extinguishers.

Maharṣi Vyāsa

This chapter about exceptions will not be complete without a mention of who we know as Vedavyāsa, the one who classified the Veda-s. His original name is Krishna Dvaipayana Vyāsa. It is because of him that the unseeable Veda-s have been classified into four texts.

It is because of him that we have the important upaniṣad-s, eighteen of the most important purāṇa-s, including the epic Mahābhārata. It is through him that Śrīmad Bhāgavatam (Bhāgavata Purāṇa), Viṣṇu Sahasranāma and the Bhagvad Gītā have manifested. It is the same Vedavyāsa who urged his father, the great ṛṣi Parāśara, to compile the Parāśara smṛti, which is the dharmaśāstra text meant for Kali Yuga. Indeed, the majority of the important texts of a Hindu are attributed to this great ṛṣi.

Yet, he was not what the śāstra-s would call a 'pure brāhmaṇa', given that his mother Satyavati was a fisherwoman and his father, the great ṛṣi Parāśara. Some versions say that Satyavati was the adopted child of a fisherman chief (Dasharaja) and the biological child of a king (Uparichara). In any case, it still means that Vedavyāsa was not entirely of pure brāhmaṇa genes, and his mother, at the time of conceiving him, was engaged in the occupation typically assigned to a vibrationally lower varṇa. So, what was the need for such a child as Vyāsa to be born to compile these foundational texts? Why didn't ṛṣi Parāśara himself do it? Surely, as a great ṛṣi, Parāśara created this child with a fisherwoman, with full awareness of the purpose of such a birth.

Interestingly, Yājñavalkya smṛti[155] talks of different jāti-s among brāhmaṇa-s and says that brāhmaṇa-s are of ten kinds: Deva (god-like), Muni (sage-like), Dvija (regenerate), Raja (king-like), Vaiśya (trader-like), Śūdra (one who does seva for others), Biḍālaka (cat-like), Paśu (beast-like), Mleccha and Caṇḍāla. The Deva Brāhmaṇa is defined as, 'He who is a professor (of religion), devoted to his religion, always content, master of his senses, and who knows the truth about the Veda-s and śāstra-s.' This seems to be the highest form of a brāhmaṇa. And the lowest is that of a Caṇḍāla Brāhmaṇa, who is defined as, 'He, who does not perform sandhya three times a day, he who does not study the Veda-s, and is devoid of other religious acts.' Somewhere in between is the Śūdra Brāhmaṇa, who

---

155 Yājñavalkya smṛti (The Mitākṣarā) Chapter 4.

is defined as 'He who lives by profession of arms or by profession of writing, or is a temple priest (arcaka), or a village priest, or runs on errands, or cooks food.'

While the śāstra-s mention varṇa as a quality obtained by birth, they also mention that by virtue of behaviour and occupation, there will be differences in vibration even among brāhmaṇa-s. We see this classification of brāhmaṇa-s even today among the Namboothiri brāhmaṇa-s of Kerala.[156]

Therefore, when we look at what Vedavyāsa contributed, he seems to be of the Śūdra Brāhmaṇa type. This is important to contemplate because had he been a pure brāhmaṇa of the highest order like his father, he might not have had the urge to write as he did. Had he been a pure śūdra (or any other pure varṇa other than brāhmaṇa), he might not have been able to perceive the unperceivable Veda-s and compile texts based on it.

All creative work, including writing, springs forth from a healthy mūlādhāra cakra, which has Śrī Brahma and Saraswati Devī as the presiding deities. Śrī Ganapathi too, who is known to have assisted Vedavyāsa in writing the Mahābhārata, is often visualised as seated in the mūlādhāra cakra. Similarly, connecting to the supreme consciousness and perceiving the highest knowledge of the Veda-s is possible only through the higher cakra-s. Thus, Vedavyāsa had to be a combination of a father who was of the highest vibration of a ṛṣi, and a mother of a lower vibration for us to receive the great texts that he compiled.

Decoding exceptions

The exceptions given in this chapter are very few, but with some details which will give us an idea of how to decode the case of an exception. In order to fully understand the case of exceptions, we

---

156 Refer https://www.namboothiri.com/articles/classification.htm for details of classification among 'Original Namboothiri-s in Kerala.'

need to be well acquainted with the science behind the rules of the dharmaśāstra texts, failing which we will miss important indicators in the stories of the lives of the exceptions. Moreover, without a knowledge of the person's previous birth and purpose in this birth, we will fall short of information.

What is most important to remember is that most cases of exceptions are not in contradiction to the śāstra-s. They happened not because they broke the rules of varṇa dharma and performed the karma of a varṇa which was not theirs, but because they took the path of bhakti and/or jñāna to its heights.

As we contemplate on who is eligible to attain the highest spiritual state, we should know that it is not just humans, but even animals, birds, demons and other beings too who can attain the highest state, by surrendering in bhakti. What better way of confirming this than the words of Bhagavān Śrī Kṛṣṇa in his final message to Uddhava, where he mentions the names of several exceptions as having attained Him through devotion alone, and not through the study of the Veda-s or by performing rituals. This is given in the following verses of the Śrīmad Bhāgavatam (11.12.3-6)

सत्सङ्गेन हि दैतेया यातुधाना मृगा: खगा: ।

गन्धर्वाप्सरसो नागा: सिद्धाश्चारणगुह्यका: ॥ ३ ॥

विद्याधरा मनुष्येषु वैश्या: शूद्रा: स्त्रियोऽन्त्यजा: ।

रजस्तम:प्रकृतयस्तस्मिंस्तस्मिन् युगे युगे ॥ ४ ॥

बहवो मत्पदं प्राप्तास्त्वाष्ट्रकायाधवादय: ।

वृषपर्वा बलिर्बाणो मयश्चाथ विभीषण: ॥ ५ ॥

सुग्रीवो हनुमानृक्षो गजो गृध्रो वणिक्पथ: ।

व्याध: कुब्जा व्रजे गोप्यो यज्ञपत्न्यस्तथापरे ॥ ६ ॥

'In every yuga, many living entities entangled in the modes of rajas and tamas (passion and ignorance) gained the association of My devotees (ṛṣi-s/saints). Thus, such living entities as the daitya-s, rākṣasa-s, birds, beasts, gandharva-s, apsara-s, nāga-s, siddha-s, cāraṇa-s, guhyaka-s and vidyādhara-s, as well as such lower (vibration) human beings as the vaiśya-s, śūdra-s, women and antyajāḥ-s (lower than śūdra varṇa), were able to achieve My supreme abode. Vṛtrāsura, Prahlāda Mahārāja and others like them also achieved My abode by association with My devotees (ṛṣi-s), as did personalities such as Vṛṣaparvā, Bali Mahārāja, Bāṇāsura, Maya (the demon), Vibhīṣaṇa, Sugrīva, Hanumān, Jāmbavān, Gajendra, Jaṭāyu, Tulādhāra, Dharma-vyādha, Kubjā, the gopīs in Vṛndāvana and the wives of the brāhmaṇa-s who were performing sacrifice.'

ते नाधीतश्रुतिगणा नोपासितमहत्तमा: ।

अव्रतातप्ततपस: मत्सङ्गान्मामुपागता: ॥ ७ ॥

'The persons I have mentioned did not undergo serious studies of the Vedic literature, nor did they worship great saintly persons, nor did they execute severe vows or austerities. Simply by association with Me and My devotees (ṛṣi-s), they attained Me.'

Chapter 8: Conclusion

Another one of the names of Devī in the Lalitā Sahasranāma is चतुःषष्टिकलामयी/catuḥṣaṣṭikalāmayi (no. 58), which means, 'She who embodies the sixty-four forms of fine arts.' When Devī Herself is the embodiment of the sixty-four arts, it is an indication that these are not mere arts serving aesthetic purposes, but instead, these are all valid methods and techniques of experiencing different aspects of Devī. These sixty-four art forms have been listed in Vātsyāyana's Kāmasūtra and were available to all, irrespective of gender or varṇa.

The most popular of these art forms are detailed in the text called Nāṭyaśāstram, which is also known as the fifth Veda or Nāṭyaveda. Bharata muni, who is credited with compiling this text, has mentioned that Nāṭyaveda, devised by Śrī Brahmā, came into origin when the devatā-s, with Indira as their head, approached Śrī Brahmā and said to him, "We want an object of diversion, which must be audible as well as visible. As the existing Veda-s are not to be listened to by those born as śūdra-s, please create another Veda which will belong equally to all the varṇa-s."[157] Thus, the Nāṭyaveda was created by Śrī Brahmā by taking portions from the other four Veda-s in the following manner:

> "The pāṭhya (recitative) he took from Ṛgveda, the song from the Sāmaveda, abhinaya (histrionic representation) from the Yajurveda and rasa (sentiments) from the Atharvaveda, and

---

157 Nāṭyaśāstram Chapter 1, verses 7 to 12. Verses 11 and 12 are given here - क्रीडनीयकमिच्छामो दृश्यं श्रव्यं च यद्भवेत् ॥11॥ न वेदव्यवहारोऽयं संश्राव्यः शूद्रजातिषु । तस्मात् सृजापरं वेदं पञ्चमं सार्ववर्णिकम् ॥ 12 ॥

thus was created the Nāṭyaveda connected with the Veda-s' principal and subsidiary (vedōpaveda), by the holy Brahmā who is omniscient."[158]

Any doubts regarding the final goal of Nāṭyaveda, in comparison to the other Veda-s, is laid to rest by the following verses in Nāṭyaśāstram:[159]

> "Those who put into practice and witness carefully the performance (of a drama) will attain the same blessed goal which masters of Vedic knowledge and performers of sacrifices (yajña) or givers of gifts (dāna) will attain, in the end."

Thus, it is technically incorrect to say that there is no Veda created for the śūdra or women when the Nāṭyaveda exists. One who is a practitioner of the traditional art forms and studies them through the lens of cakra-s and the knowledge of yoga can discover a whole new spiritual path that encompasses the very teachings of the four Veda-s, in practical form, suitable to everyone. For example, in comparing yoga and the classical dance form of Bharatanāṭyam, an article titled 'Bharatanāṭyam and Yoga',[160] mentions:

> "The sixth step of Aṣṭāṅga Yoga is dhāraṇā or concentration. This concentration, when taken to its extreme, leads us into the meditative state of dhyāna. Many of the concentrative practices of yoga are based on the mandala-s that are

---

158 Nāṭyaśāstram Chapter 1, verses 17 & 18. जग्राह पाठ्यमृग्वेदात् सामभ्यो गीतमेव च । यजुर्वेदादभिनयान् रसानाथर्वणादपि॥ 17 ॥ वेदोपवेदैः संबद्धो नाट्यवेदो महात्मना । एवं भगवता सृष्टो ब्रह्मणा सर्ववेदिना ॥ 18

159 Nāṭyaśāstram Chapter XXXVI, verses 77 to 79. Verses 78 & 79 are given here - य इदं श्रुणुयान्नित्यं प्रोक्तञ्चेदं स्वयम्भुवा । प्रयोगं यच्च कुर्वीत प्रेक्षते चावधानवान्॥78॥ या गतिर्वेदविदुषां या गतिर्यज्ञकारिणः। या गतिर्दानशीलानां तां गतिं प्राप्नुयान्नरः ॥ 79॥

160 Article: 'Bharatanatyam And Yoga' by Yogacharya Dr. Ananda Balayogi Bhavanani and Yogacharini Smt. Devasena Bhavanani | Yoganjali Natyalayam, Pondicherry-13, South India

assigned to the different elements of the manifest universe. Bharatanāṭyam utilises numerous shapes that are similar to the mandala-s of Yoga and Yantra, and these shapes also produce a bio-electromagnetic field that energises not only the dancer but also her audience...

The dancer requires a similar state of utmost concentration in order to bring about the union of bhāva, rāga and tāla in her presentation. The different aspects of Bharatanāṭyam, such as nṛtta, nṛtya and nātya, must be seamlessly unified with great concentrative ability for the performance to peak in its intensity. When the dancer achieves that peak of concentration in her performance, she loses herself in a state of meditation. The yogic state of dhyāna and the trance-like states experienced by the dancers while performing are quite similar in their universal nature. Śrī Tiruvenkatachari, an eminent dance historian (1887), compared Yoga with dance and said that the secret is 'forgetfulness of the individual self.' He also mentioned that dance is a means of attaining mokṣa just as is yoga."

Classical Bhāratiya dance, music and drama based on Nāṭyaśāstram, traditional paintings based on Śilpaśāstram and architecture based on Vāstuśāstram are some of the forms of the sixty-four arts, which are still in existence today. Interested readers, and especially practitioners, should explore these art forms as mokṣa śāstra-s, rediscovering these as valid paths of self-realisation.

The saṃskṛtam words mentioned by Pāṇini, which refer to a female teacher (ācāryānī), a female student (adhyetrī), a female novice (māṇavikā), hostels for female students (chhātri-śālā), etc.,[161] are likely to be with respect to the learning centres of these art forms, rather than Vedic gurukuls where girls studied Vedic chanting (as

---

161 India As Known To Pāṇini, Chapter III, Section 4.

assumed by some people). We have seen that even when the case of brahmavādini-s is mentioned as studying Veda-s in another kalpa, there, too, it is mentioned that they had to undertake the study at home, taught by their father, paternal uncle or elder brother. Students of history should note that whenever there is doubt about the historical basis of a fact pertaining to Sanātana Dharma, such as whether or not girls went to Vedic gurukuls with boys, the doubt should be clarified by a deeper understanding of the subtle science. In this case, we should note that the bodies of girls of menstrual age could not have withstood the high vibrations of Vedic chants, and therefore, they would not have been encouraged to study in Vedic gurukuls where the boys chanted.

Most importantly, we should stop trying to see the Vedic period as what we want it to be because our understanding is really limited, not to mention heavily socially conditioned. Instead, there must always be an effort to raise ourselves to the level of the śāstra-s, with a willingness to let go of our preconceived notions. For many of us, having led lives that are quite different from that prescribed by the śāstra-s, there is the added layer of rebellion springing from guilt, which creates within us resistance to even know the truth.

What we are should not come in the way of realising what we need to be. This is, after all, the Kali Yuga; mistakes do happen. Genuine repentance, with a pledge to respect the śāstra-s and live in accordance with it as far as possible, will create the much-needed lightness within. They say that the spiritual path requires great courage. Indeed, as Guru-s say, it takes courage to be brutally honest with oneself, examine one's actions without judgement, and still find the compassion within to forgive.

Never doubt that every text that sprung from the Veda-s, be it the śāstra-s, purāṇa-s or tantra, is fair and just to all people in all its injunctions. When a civilisation thinks of material goals as its measure of success, that is when the rules come under sociology because they are man-made and unfair to the weak. This is not the case with Sanātana dharma, where the rules are based on biology, with the goal of spiritual upliftment and attainment of mokṣa, for every individual. This idea is powerfully expressed in the following words of Swami Vivekananda:

> "And may I ask you, Europeans, what country have you ever raised to better conditions? Wherever you have found weaker races, you have exterminated them by the roots, as it were. You have settled on their lands, and they are gone forever. What is the history of your America, your Australia, and New Zealand, your Pacific islands and South Africa? Where are those aboriginal races there today? They are all exterminated. You have killed them outright as if they were wild beasts. It is only where you have not the power to do so, and there only that other nations are still alive.
>
> The object of the peoples of Europe is to exterminate all in order to live themselves. The aim of the Aryans is to raise all up to their own level, nay, even to a higher level than themselves. The means of European civilisation is the sword. Of the Aryans, the division into different varṇa-s. This system of division into different varṇa-s is the stepping-stone to civilisation, making one rise higher and higher in proportion to one's learning and culture. In Europe, it is everywhere: victory to the strong and death to the weak. In the land of Bhārat, every social rule is for the protection of the weak."

'In the land of Bhārat, every social rule is for the protection of the weak.' We will find this to be true every single time we make the journey to explore the subtle science behind the seemingly unfair rules in the śāstra. This thought should penetrate the mind of every person who attempts to decode the rules in the śāstra, and with all humility, we must ask the divine ṛṣi-s to reveal the truth behind the rules they framed. And even if we fail to understand the deeper meaning of

some rules, let us follow them anyway. The examples of explanations given in this book are intended to build in us the needed faith to trust the word of the śāstra-s even when our intellect might fail to understand it.

Are brāhmaṇa-s a privileged class?

The people of Bhārat have passed through that most difficult period of cultural guilt when the colonisers sought to break us from within by breaking the source of our strength. The silent strength of this culture has been the purity of the brāhmaṇa varṇa, whose austerity and resulting aura protected all the vibrationally weaker ones. By nurturing the idea that the brāhmaṇa varṇa is a privileged class which enjoys many benefits and a self-imposed superior status looking down upon the other varṇa-s, the outsiders sought to break this culture from within. It was even said that the dharmaśāstra-s were written by brāhmaṇa-s to favour themselves. It is this idea that continues to rear its ugly head in all the forms of caste-based activism that we see even today. Therefore, let us be clear about the so-called privileges of the brāhmaṇa varṇa, as ordained in the dharmaśāstra texts through the words of Mahāperiyavā, as he explains a day in the life of a brāhmaṇa:

> "A brāhmaṇa must wake up two hours before sunrise (Brahma muhūrtha). After getting up, he cleans his teeth, bathes in cold water and performs sandhyāvandana and japa. Next, he goes through aupāsana and agnihotra. These rites come under 'devayajña.' Next is 'brahmayajña', the daily study and chanting of the Veda-s. As part of this rite, there are some tarpaṇa-s (libations) to be offered. This happens in the first part of the daytime.
>
> In the second part of the daytime, the brāhmaṇa must teach his disciples the Veda-s — this is adhyāpana. Afterwards, he must gather flowers himself for the pūjā he is

to perform. Since he is not expected to earn a salary — and if he does not own any land received as a gift — he must beg for his food and also for the material for the conduct of various sacrifices. The brāhmaṇa has a right to beg, but it is a restrictive right because it means he can take only the minimum needed for the upkeep and what is required for the performance of rituals. A considerable part of what he receives as gifts is to be paid as dakshina to the priests officiating the sacrifices he performs.

After the second part of the day and a portion of the third has thus been spent, the brāhmaṇa must bathe again and perform mādhyāhnika. Next, he does pitṛ tarpana, and this rite is followed by homa and pūja. It will now be mid-day, and the fourth part of daytime will have been over, and the brāhmaṇa must have completed the rites meant for the deities, the Veda-s and the pitṛ-s. Two more rites remain, which are manuṣya yajña (feeding guests) and bhūtayajña, which includes bali to the creatures of the earth and the poor (Vaiśvadeva rite). Rice is offered in the sacrificial fire and also as bali. It is only after all this that the brāhmaṇa can have his (first) meal at around 1.00 PM. Until then, he must not take anything except some milk or buttermilk, but never coffee or any snacks. If he has any other sacrifices to conduct, pāka, havir, or sōma, his mealtime would be further delayed. If he has a sraddha to perform, he will have to eat later than usual.

After his meal, a brāhmaṇa must read the purāṇa-s. Next, he has the duty of teaching members of other varṇa their hereditary vocations, arts and crafts. His calling is that of a teacher, and he must not do any other job......There is also proof of the impartiality of the dharmaśāstra-s in that the brāhmaṇa, who is expected to be proficient in all the arts and branches of learning, can only give instruction in them but cannot take up any for his livelihood, however lucrative it be and however less demanding than the pursuit of the Vedic dharma.

He does not have a moment of rest or relaxation, for soon it will be time for his evening bath, sandhyāvandana, sacrifices and japa. Vaiśvadeva has to be performed at night before he takes his meal and retires to bed. On most nights, he takes only light food consisting of fruits, milk, etc. On Ekādashi, he has to fast the whole day.

There is not a moment without work. It is clear that if the brāhmaṇa created the śāstra-s, it is not because he wanted to live a life of ease and comfort. On the contrary, the śāstra-s impose on him a life of hardship and austerity, a life of utter physical and mental discipline.

Further, he has a handicap which he does not share with others. If he believes that he is superior to others because he does intellectual work, he will only be a hindrance to himself."[162]

It is through the purity of brāhmaṇa-s that the rest of the society is protected and raised vibrationally. To render this service to society, the śāstra-s ordain a brāhmaṇa to go through tremendous hardship, with no right to physical rest, proper mealtimes or even what we today consider a basic human right to earn a livelihood out of the vast knowledge and skills that he acquires. The yajña-s he performs are also for the sake of others. Fame, wealth, comfort — a brāhmaṇa has to deny himself all these so that he remains vibrationally pure in thought and actions to be of help to others. Those of other varṇa-s who fight for the right to have the same vocation as that of a brāhmaṇa should first attempt to live the life of a brāhmaṇa.

---

162 Voice of God, Volume 2, chapters titled 'Brahmins and non-Brhamins', 'A day in the life of a Brahmin', and 'Brahmins are not a privileged jati.'

Which varṇa is more blessed in the kali yuga?

Yes, there is some unfairness in kali yuga as to which varṇa is more blessed and, therefore, has greater chances of succeeding in the spiritual journey. Take a guess as to which varṇa that might be, and then read the words of Mahārṣi Vyāsa, who explained this in the Viṣṇu Purāṇa (VI. 2) when sages approached him with the question 'In what age does a little dharma yield very great rewards?'

The story goes that when the sages asked him this question, Vyāsa was bathing in the Ganges; he came out and uttered, *'Śūdra is good, and Kali is good'*, and then again plunged into the river; then he again came out and said, *'Well done, O Śūdra! You are blessed'*; he again plunged into the river, came out and said, *'Women are good and blessed; who is more blessed than they!'* When he finished his bath and after he performed his morning rites, the sages asked him to explain what he meant by calling Kali, śūdra-s and women good and blessed. He replied,

> "A man secures in a single day and night in the Kali Yuga as much reward of tapas, celibacy and japa as is obtained in ten years in Kṛta yuga, in one year in Tretà yuga and in a month in Dvāpara yuga; therefore, I spoke of Kali as good. In Kali yuga, a man secures merely by the glorification or incessant repetition of the name of Keśava what he would secure by deep meditation in Kṛta, by sacrifices in Treta, and by worship in Dvāpara; I am pleased with Kali because a man secures great eminence of dharma with a little effort.
>
> Persons of the three higher varṇa-s have to study the Veda-s after observing many strict rules, and then they have to perform sacrifices which require wealth; they incur sin if they do not perform their duties properly; they cannot eat and drink as they please, but are dependent on the observance of many rules as to food etc. Dvija-s secure higher worlds after great trouble; (whereas), the śūdra secures

his worlds by serving the three varṇa-s, he has the right to offer the pākayajña (without mantra-s), and therefore, he is more blessed than a dvija. He (a śūdra) has not to observe strict rules about proper and disallowed food or drink, and therefore, he was declared as most good by me.

A woman, by serving her husband in thought, word, and deed, secures with less trouble the same worlds that her husband secures with great effort and trouble, and therefore, I said a third time about women that they were blessed.

The acquisition of dharma is secured with small trouble by men who wash off all their sins by the water in the form of the qualities of their soul; śūdra-s do the same by being intent on service to dvija-s and women also secure the same without trouble by service to their husbands. Therefore, all these three are regarded by me as most blessed."[163]

If there is anything that readers of this book must agree upon by now, it is that no individual is denied the path to mokṣa, as per the dharmaśāstra. Several rules in the śāstra-s have been misconstrued in the name of equality understood from the Western perspective. From the lens of the śāstra-s, equality means making available equally

---

163 Some of the verses are quoted here, vide Dr. P.V. Kane 'History of Dharmasastra' Volume V, Part II:

ध्यायन्कृते यजन्यज्ञैस्त्रेतायां द्वापारेऽर्चयन् । यदाप्नोति तदाप्नोति कलौ संकीर्त्य केशवम् । धर्मोत्कर्षमतीवात्र प्राप्नोति पुरुषः कलौ । अल्पायासेन धर्मज्ञास्तेन तुष्टोस्म्यहं कलेः ॥ "जयन्ति ते निजाँल्लोकान् क्लेशेन महता द्विजाः । द्विजशुश्रूषयैवैष पाकयज्ञाधिकारवान् । निजाञ्जयति वै लोकान् शुद्रो धन्यतरस्ततः ॥ भक्ष्याभक्ष्येषु नास्यारित पेयापेयेषु वै यतः । नियमो मुनि- शार्दूलास्तेनासौ साध्वितीरितः । "योषिच्छुश्रूषणाद्भर्तुः कर्मणा मनसा गिरा । तद्विता शुभमाप्नोति तत्सालोक्यं यतो द्विजाः ॥ नातिक्लेशेन महता तानेव पुरुषो यथा । तृतीयं व्याहृतं तेन मया साध्विति योषितः ॥ स्वल्पेन हि प्रयत्नेन धर्मः सिध्यति वै कलौ । नरैरात्मगुणाम्भोभिः क्षालित।खिलकल्बिषैः॥ शूद्रैश्च द्विजशुश्रूषा तत्परैर्द्विजसत्तमाः । तथा स्त्रीभिरनायासात् पति- शुश्रूपयैव हि । ततस्त्रितयमप्येतन्मम धन्यतरं मतम् । धर्मसम्पादने क्लेशो द्विजातीनां कृतादिषु ॥ विष्णुपु० VI. 2. 17-18, 22-24, 28-29, 34-36.

valid paths for each individual to fulfil the purpose of their birth while moving towards the attainment of mokṣa. For this to happen, there are different rules for individuals owing to the differences in every individual's biological makeup. The mistake we often make is assuming that one path is superior to another when, in fact, specific paths prescribed for a specific set of individuals are equal in their ability to take the seeker towards the final goal of mokṣa. The customised path prescribed for a specific set of individuals is also the shortest and easiest path for them, whereas imitating another's path makes the journey longer and, at times, dangerous.

Finally, what cannot be communicated through the limitations of language and modern science can only be communicated through the experience of practitioners, bringing alive the injunctions in the śāstra-s. Therefore, to fully comprehend the rules in the śāstra-s, we must become practitioners of the smṛti-s; or, in Periyavā's words, smārta.

Acknowledgements

This book has been made possible because of the direct and indirect support and blessings of many individuals. Mention must be made of the following people, without whose support this book might have turned out quite different.

I sincerely thank the group of volunteers: Kum. Aiswarya P.L, Dr. Sriram Devanathan, Śrī Vijay Balachandran, Smt. Vineeta Govindasamy, Śrī Niranjan Aravind, Śrī Madhusudan Padmanabhan, Kum. Kiruthika Vinaya, Smt. Falguni Shah, Smt. Hamsini Murthy and Śrī Udaya Bhaskar Guda for their research inputs and support with resources such as books and reading material.

Special mention must be made of Kum. Aiswarya P.L who tirelessly helped in the translation of several of the śāstra-s rules with the help of Śrī Vignesh Somayaji and Śrī V. Krishna Sharma, to whom I offer sincere gratitude. Special thanks also to Dr. Sriram Devanathan, who supported by providing important published research papers cited in this book.

Gratitude must be expressed to Śrī Niranjan Aravind, who kindly gifted the six volumes of the 'Voice of God' series, which became the starting point for this book. Thanks also to Śrī Udaya Bhaskar Guda and Bhandarkar Oriental Research Institute for gifting the five important volumes of books on 'History of Dharmaśāstra' by Dr. P.V. Kane, which made a compilation of the śāstra rules a lot easier than I had imagined.

Words cannot express the gratitude and credit that goes to the enlightened Masters who have blessed this work and wish to remain anonymous. It is their goodness, compassion and patience to teach a work-in-progress like me which made this book possible.

And to the Divine Mother who made me an instrument of Her Will, I bow in servitude.